LITERARY DISEASES

Literary Diseases

Theme and Metaphor in the Italian Novel

by GIAN-PAOLO BIASIN

UNIVERSITY OF TEXAS PRESS, AUSTIN AND LONDON

Grateful acknowledgment is made for permission to quote from the
following:

Confessions of Zeno, by Italo Svevo. Copyright © 1930, and renewed
1958 by Alfred A. Knopf, Inc.
Le meraviglie d'Italia: Gli anni, by Carlo Emilio Gadda. Copyright © 1964 by Giulio Einaudi Editore, S.p.A., Torino.
One, None and a Hundred-thousand, by Luigi Pirandello. Copyright
© 1933 by the Pirandello Estate.
Una peccatrice e altri romanzi, by Giovanni Verga. Copyright ©
1965 by Arnoldo Mondadori Editor.

Library of Congress Cataloging in Publication Data

Biasin, Gian-Paolo.
    Literary diseases.

    Bibliography: p.
    Includes index.
    1. Italian literature—History and criticism.
2. Diseases in literature. 3. Mental illness in
literature. I. Title.
PQ4053.D5B5   853'.03   74–30345
ISBN 0-292-74614-8

For Maria Rita,
precious image of happiness and health

CONTENTS

A NOTE OF ACKNOWLEDGMENT

The idea for this book originated in Karl-Ludwig Selig's proposal that I give a paper at the Romance Section of the Modern Language Association meeting in December 1967, held in New York. Subsequently, I devoted my constant attention to the subject and published some partial results of my research in *Modern Language Notes*, *Belfagor*, *Modern Fiction Studies*, *Paragone*, and *Lingua e stile*.

I wish to thank Ezio Raimondi for the friendly discussions, valuable suggestions, and generous encouragement that helped this book assume its present form. A grateful thought, too, for much the same reason, to my friends Ciriaco Moròn-Arroyo, Rupert Roopnaraine, Pietro Pucci, and Richard Macksey.

Other useful suggestions came from Giovanni Sinicropi and Wolfgang Holdheim; Anthony Caputi and Linda Hutcheon helped with my English. To them and to the Cornell students who enlivened these pages and these years with their presence and enthusiasm, my gratitude.

LITERARY DISEASES

To be sure, health is the only admissible ideal, to which the one I consider a man has a right to aspire; but, when health is given immediately to a human being, it hides half of the world from him.

Jacques Rivière,
letter to Antonin Artaud

1. From Anatomy to Criticism

A work is not only a consequence of the past already lived but also a future inventing itself, an original act concluded within itself.

Ezio Raimondi, "Symbolic Criticism"

Considering how common illness is, how tremendous the spiritual change that it brings, how astonishing, when the lights of health go down, the undiscovered countries that are then disclosed, what wastes and deserts of the soul a slight attack of influenza brings to view, what precipices and lawns sprinkled with bright flowers a little rise of temperature reveals, what ancient and obdurate oaks are uprooted in us by the act of sickness, how we go down into the pit of death and feel the waters of annihilation close above our heads and wake thinking to find ourselves in the presence of the angels and the harpers when we have a tooth out and come to the surface in the dentist's armchair and confuse his "Rinse the mouth—rinse the mouth" with the greeting of the Deity stooping from the floor of Heaven to welcome us—when we think of this, as we are so frequently forced to think of it, it becomes strange indeed that illness has not taken its place with love and battle and jealousy among the prime themes of literature. Novels, one would have thought, would have been devoted to influenza; epic poems to typhoid; odes to pneumonia; lyrics to toothache. But no; with a few exceptions—De Quincey attempted something of the sort in *The Opium Eater*; there must be a volume or two about disease scattered through the pages of Proust—literature does its best to maintain that its concern is with the mind; that the body is a sheet of plain glass through which the soul looks straight and clear, and, save for one or two passions such as desire and greed, is null, and negligible and non-existent. On the contrary, the very opposite is true.[1]

Virginia Woolf's words, elegant as always and seemingly unstudied,

[1] Virginia Woolf, "On Being Ill," in *Collected Essays*, IV, 193.

are a good introduction to our essay. To her acknowledgment of the importance of the body (an acknowledgment that harkens back to Arthur Schopenhauer and Friedrich Nietzsche), we must immediately add that disease actually is a prime theme of literature, although it has not been sufficiently recognized as such by readers and critics alike; that, therefore, many other names should be added to those of Thomas De Quincey and Marcel Proust; and, finally, that literature, while being concerned with bodily phenomena, will always tend to transform these according to its own procedures and norms.[2]

In the writer's quest for the world, man, and truth (a truth), he neglects no aspect of experience; even the most banal or secondary one acquires its well-defined meaning at a cultural, historical, existential, and structural level. Each of these aspects, to the very degree that it is absorbed into the literary universe, is transformed into images, themes, and *topoi* through which reality is perceived, organized, and ultimately known.

One of these themes, a very ancient one, concerns disease, which is part of life and often an announcement of death, both an individual fact and a social datum: Philoctetes and Prince André, Hercules *furens* and Orlando *furioso*, the *dame aux camélias* and Henry IV, Madame Merteuil and Zeno, and the plagues described by Giovanni Boccaccio, Alessandro Manzoni, and Albert Camus (in differing coordinates of time and space) are included in this theme. Outside literature, one remembers Leonardo da Vinci's anatomical drawings or El Greco's figures modeled after Toledo's madmen in the insane asylum (according to Gregorio Marañon);[3] then, following the macabre-scientific combination peculiar to the anatomies of the seventeenth century, one can cite the Dutch physician Friedrich Ruysch and his true-to-life mummies that were to inspire Giacomo Leopardi later on or Francesco Susini's intriguing anatomical waxes

---

[2] In *L'univers médical de Proust*, Henri Béhar examines the way in which the physiological becomes a reverberation of inner life; Proust is presented as the neurologist of Europe's malaise at the beginning of this century. On disease in literature, see also Egon Friedell, "Das Zwanzigste Jahrhundert" and "Das neue Ungehüm," in *Aphorismen und Briefe.*

[3] Gregorio Marañon, *El Greco y Toledo.*

in Florence's Specola Museum. It is also interesting to note how, according to Raymond Klibanski, Erwin Panofsky, and Fritz Saxl, the leper became a figurative *topos* in Albrecht Dürer's painting.[4] (But a history of how many leper hospitals were transformed into insane asylums and of the underlying reasons for such a phenomenon has yet to be written, notwithstanding the chapter on "the great imprisonment" in Michel Foucault's *Raison et déraison: Histoire de la folie à l'âge classique.*)[5]

At any rate, today the dichotomy between sane and sick, normal and pathological seems to be predominant in scientific, sociological, and moral thought, as well as in the average man's typical mental attitudes. In a recent interview, Foucault stated: "Every society establishes a whole series of systems of oppositions—between good and evil, permitted and prohibited, lawful and illicit, criminal and non-criminal, etc. All of these oppositions, which are constitutive of society, today in Europe are being reduced to the simple opposition between normal and pathological. This opposition not only is simpler than others, but also has the advantage of letting us believe there is a technique to bring the pathological back to normal."[6] On this side of the Atlantic, Susan Sontag wrote in an essay, somewhat peremptorily, "Ours is an age which consciously pursues health, and yet only believes in the reality of sickness."[7]

If we turn to consider the origin of today's disturbing scene, we

[4] Raymond Klibanski, Erwin Panofsky, and Fritz Saxl, *Saturn and Melancholy: Studies in the History of Natural Philosophy, Religion and Art.* In *The Life and Art of Albrecht Dürer*, Erwin Panofsky also examines "Melencolia I" and shows how the artist's melancholy is the result of a merging of the neo-Platonic theory on genius with German mysticism; with due reservations, he states that melancholy becomes what could be called a protoromantic interpretation of art (pp. 156–171 and 282).

[5] Michel Foucault, *Madness and Civilization: A History of Insanity in the Age of Reason.*

[6] Paolo Caruso (ed.), *Conversazioni con Lévi-Strauss, Foucault, Lacan,* pp. 95–98. See also Georges Canguilhem, *Sain et pathologique* and *Essai sur quelques problèmes concernant le normal et le pathologique.*

[7] Susan Sontag, *Against Interpretation,* p. 49; and on p. 50: "Kleist, Kierkegaard, Nietzsche, Dostoevski, Kafka, Baudelaire, Rimbaud, Genet, Simone Weil—have their authority with us precisely because of their air of unhealthiness."

are likely to find it in the Romantic Movement, especially if we accept Morse Peckham's idea, developed from the views of Arthur Lovejoy and René Welleck, that the major revolutionary discovery of the romantics was the conception of reality as "organicism," as a "dynamic organicism" (rather than as a preordained "mechanism").[8] Disease is inherent in an organism. So is vitality, and so are evil and death. To give an example, Leopardi's description of a garden as a "hospital" of suffering beings can be taken as emblematic of a whole poetry that fully expresses the dichotomy between the recognition of the negativity of the universe, on one side, and the irreducible vitality and sentiments of the poet, on the other; according to Sergio Solmi's conclusions, "his wound had to remain open."[9] This metaphorical "wound" seems precisely what G. W. F. Hegel diagnosed as "the Romantic malady of his age" according to Erich Heller: "a severance of mind from world, soul from circumstance, human inwardness from external condition."[10] This "Romantic malady" can be considered the very root of today's alienation.[11]

Turning now to the development of medicine as a scientific, social, and historic background of literature, one fact stands out: the scientific attitude toward death as a source of vital knowledge is paralleled in romantic literature by an analogous evaluation of death as a factor of individuality. Often the death of a romantic hero who has been sick with that most spiritual of diseases, tuberculosis, represents an affirmation of his exceptionality, of his spirituality. The *dame aux camélias* and Violetta in *La traviata* are indeed exemplary for the characterization of their epoch. In them the romantic tendency to equate passionate love with disease appears quite clearly. (Of course, I am omitting other characteristic and important attitudes, such as melancholy and sadness, because they are less ex-

[8] Morse Peckham, *The Triumph of Romanticism*; see also idem, *Beyond the Tragic Vision*, and idem, *Romanticism: The Culture of the 19th Century*.

[9] Sergio Solmi, *Scritti leopardiani*, p. 107.

[10] Erich Heller, *The Artist's Journey into the Interior*, p. 103.

[11] On today's alienation, see David Caute, *The Illusion: An Essay on Politics, Theatre and the Novel*, p. 164: "Consider two types of alienation, the one a noxious disease, the other an antidote, a vaccine to the virus," the one social, the other artistic.

treme and less directly related to the theme under examination.)[12]

On the other hand, the romantic period also considered disease and death as punishments with a moral or divine character; one thinks of Madame Merteuil's smallpox in *Les liaisons dangereuses* or of Don Rodrigo's plague in *Fermo e Lucia* (then in *I promessi sposi,* with a less obvious interpretation). In these instances the scientific data were used in an unscientific, almost metaphysical way that did not have much to do with a faithful rendering in literature of actual medical progress, perhaps because the latter remained in the isolated world of clinics for a long time.

However, as Albert Béguin reminds us in *Le Romantisme Allemand,* disease had an importance for certain romantics that can only be fully recognized today, in the light of the literary developments of the late nineteenth century.[13] The most profoundly romantic disease was intimately linked with knowledge and artistic creation in a rich and ambiguous relationship. For instance, in Novalis's *Fragmente* one reads: "Likely, diseases are the stimulus and the most interesting subject for our meditation and activity. . . . Only, we know little the art of using them"; "Medicine must transform itself into the doctrine of the art of living"; "Diseases should be considered as bodily madness and, partially, as fixed ideas"; "Life is a malady of the spirit, since in it one hopes with passion. . . . Death is the principle that makes our life romantic. Death is—life. Through death life is reinforced"; "Every disease is a musical problem, healing is a musical solution"; "If a man began to love disease or sorrow, the most exciting pleasure would penetrate him"; "Poetry is the great art of constructing transcendental sanity. Therefore the poet is a transcendental physician"; "Could disease not be a means of higher synthesis?"[14]

Even though such thoughts seem not to have found a large and immediate following, they did have implications and consequences that were fundamental for the nineteenth century. On the one

[12] Cf. José Deleito y Piñuela, *El sentimiento de tristeza en la literatura contemporánea,* and Jean Starobinski, *A History of Medicine.*

[13] Albert Béguin, *Le Romantisme Allemand.*

[14] Novalis, *Fragmente,* in *Schriften,* III, passim.

hand, they are a prelude first to Schopenhauer's and Nietzsche's philosophic interest in biological matters, then to naturalism and the emphasis on scientific knowledge of disease. On the other hand, they foreshadow a whole morbid trend that leads through J. C. F. Hölderlin and Gérard de Nerval to symbolism, decadence, and, ultimately, Antonin Artaud's and Raymond Roussel's literature of the irrational.

The scientifically generic and poetically vague way in which the romantics treated the theme of disease was replaced after the second half of the nineteenth century by a cold and precise, clinical and positivist tone. Disease-passion inexorably became physical illness in all its terrible concreteness and painful evidence; disease-punishment disappeared along with what J. Hillis Miller, echoing Nietzsche, has called "the disappearance of God" or at any rate with the fading of the interest in transcendence. No longer a punishment, it remained pure and simple disease, whether physical or (especially later on) psychic, so that from Sigmund Freud's discoveries a wholly new morality was born, one based on the dynamics of the guilt complex.[15] The death of Emma Bovary, described by Gustave Flaubert with relentless clinical attention to the painful and cruel symptoms of poisoning, dramatically marked the end of the romantic hero in France, while in Italy something similar occurred a few years later with the death of Narcisa Valderi in Giovanni Verga's *Una peccatrice*.[16]

From then on, disease was dealt with more and more extensively and frequently in literature. The naturalists, under the impulse of positivism and with the purpose of scientific research, focused their attention not so much on inner, individual aspects of reality as on outer, social ones (in the direction foreshadowed by Novalis), not so much on moods as on this or that atmosphere. As a consequence, their major interest was in the poorest class of the population, its

[15] J. Hillis Miller, *The Disappearance of God*; cf. some relevant pages by the Norwegian physician and writer Knut Hamsun, *Psychologie und Dichtung*.

[16] Recall the final words of Charles Augustin Sainte-Beuve's famous review of *Madame Bovary*: "Son and brother of distinguished physicians, Mr. Gustave Flaubert holds his pen as others the scalpel. Anatomists and physiologists, I find you everywhere!" (*Causeries du Lundi*, XIII, 363).

miserable living conditions in urban slums (those of Paris were famous), and certain typical illnesses transmitted from one generation to the next by heredity (like the hereditary madness in Émile Zola's *La bête humaine,* a truly social as well as literary document). The results were works in which the most realistic details of a given sickness were described carefully, technically, and, more often than not, morbidly; it is well known that Zola said he was inspired by a treatise on experimental medicine by Claude Bernard. (I would emphasize "experimental" even more than "medicine.") His statement can enlighten us about the type of interest, substantial and methodological, of literature in medicine from the middle of the last century.[17]

In Italy, the industrial revolution, although somewhat delayed, brought developments analogous with those that had occurred in France and England and bearing similar consequences in the literary field.[18] The *veristi* writers, however, in general abstained from the representation of the most extreme aspects of a pathological nature, yet the lesson of naturalism was deeply felt and left its mark upon the Italian cultural milieu. Verga's restraint whenever he describes the agony and death of one of the characters in his mature novels—from La Longa to Mastro-don Gesualdo—remains exemplary; so does Luigi Capuana's in his description of pathological cases, from Giacinta to Eugenia.

On the contrary, the Milanese group of *Scapigliati* often indulged in an exasperated and morbid representation of illness. By taking up again melancholy (of the Adolphe type) and Novalis's romantic disease, they in fact anticipated a certain tendency of literature at the end of the nineteenth century—the tendency toward decadence (and even to G. A. Borgese's *Rubè*), which has its roots in this direct relationship between literature and medicine.[19]

[17] Cf. Reino Virtanen, "Claude Bernard and the History of Ideas," in *Claude Bernard and Experimental Medicine,* ed. Maurice B. Visscher and Francisco Grande, pp. 9–23; also Donald G. Charlton, *Positivist Thought in France during the Second Empire, 1852–1870,* pp. 72–85.

[18] Cf. Gian Franco Venè, *Letteratura e capitalismo in Italia dal '700 ad oggi,* now *Il capitale e il poeta.*

[19] Disease in *Rubè* as an abandonment to the irrational is treated by Mario

Foucault has clearly shown how a whole line of clinical studies in the late 1800's was oriented toward the concept and the status of "degeneration," a concept that some physicians had utilized "to characterize the weakening of the robust human naturalness, condemned by society, civilization, laws, and language to a life of artifices and diseases." Such a negative stance was to be reversed only gradually by medical science, starting with Xavier Bichat: "At the very beginning of life, degeneration is the necessity of death, from which it is indissociable, and the most general possibility of sickness. The structural link between this concept and the anatomo-pathologic method appears now clearly. In the perception of anatomy, death was the high point of view from which disease opened upon its own truth; the trinity life-disease-death was articulated in a triangle whose top was death."[20] It is interesting to note the extraordinary cultural coincidence between degeneration as a negative medical concept and degeneration as a philosophic conception in the works of Schopenhauer, Nietzsche, Paul Bourget, and Max Nordau. An entire area of European culture is usually designated, perhaps a bit too conventionally, by the name of "decadence." In Italy the most important and up-to-date representative of this trend was Gabriele D'Annunzio, whose sensitivity to the theme of physical decadence, disease, and death was not accidental. In France, a similar attitude can be found in Joris-Karl Huysman's *À rebours*.[21]

Examples from D'Annunzio's works are innumerable, but two

Isnenghi, "Borgese, Jahier e la guerra," *Quaderni piacentini* 5, no. 27 (June 1966): 80–90; in particular, p. 84: "The willful sense of success and power is imbued with an anxiety of self-destruction: war, disease, sleep, prison, death, are conditions that are continuously assimilated and indiscriminately sought by Rubè. They constitute his awareness, they mark his historically exemplary value."

[20] Michel Foucault, *Naissance de la clinique: Une archéologie du regard médical*, pp. 157 and 159; also, see A. E. Carter, *The Idea of Decadence in French Literature, 1830–1900*.

[21] One might recall the Spanish novelist Ramón del Valle-Inclán for the same type of sensitivity, especially in *Sonata de otoño*. On literary decadence in general, see Francesco Flora, "Il decadentismo," in *Questioni e correnti di storia letteraria*, ed. Attilio Momigliano, pp. 761–810.

will suffice. One is taken from the early short story "Il cerusico di mare": "The following day the cuticle of the tumor was swollen by a bloody serum and broke. The whole part took on the appearance of a wasp's nest, from where purulent materials gushed out abundantly. The inflammation and the suppuration were deepening and extending rapidly."[22] The second example is from the late *Il compagno dagli occhi senza cigli* and seems to illustrate clearly the link between D'Annunzio and Novalis: "Disease and death are the two blindfolded Muses that lead us in silence to discover the spirituality of forms."[23] Between these two examples, one could of course add famous pages from *Il piacere, Il fuoco,* or *Il notturno.*

But, concurrently with the pseudoscientific incorporation of medical data in naturalist literature, which sought to master pathology in order to understand the world better, toward the end of the nineteenth century an equally important phenomenon occurred. Medicine evolved radically in a particular field, that of mental illnesses, and these diseases became the focus of predominant interest. Foucault has shown that those who were mad were kept in a status of social and cultural freedom until circa 1650. However, during the seventeenth century they were isolated and burdened with a more or less marked sense of guilt, and this attitude lasted precisely until the end of the nineteenth century.[24] Cesare Lombroso, even with his efforts to liberalize the treatment of madmen, idiots, and criminals, is perhaps the most dramatic and saddest example of a whole social and clinical trend on which Michel David has made pungent re-

[22] Gabriele D'Annunzio, "Il cerusico di mare," in *Le novelle della Pescara,* pp. 371–385.

[23] Gabriele D'Annunzio, *Prose di ricerca, di lotta, etc.,* p. 613. The harking back to Novalis is explicit on p. 623: "When did I read that every sickness is a musical problem?" and in "Libro segreto" as well, p. 877. Cf. Ezio Raimondi, "Gabriele D'Annunzio," in *Il Novecento,* vol. 9 of *Storia della letteratura italiana,* ed. Emilio Cecchi and Natalino Sapegno, pp. 1–84, particularly p. 77: "Perhaps in the orphic mirror of a celebrating language that multiplied the masks of Eros, the nocturnal shadow of a great refusal remained as if suspended between the 'blindfolded Muses' of disease and death."

[24] Michel Foucault, *Maladie mentale et psychologie;* but an earlier periodization is documented in Marañon, *El Greco y Toledo.*

marks and that, unfortunately, persists even today, notwithstanding a few exceptions.[25]

In the field of mental illness there had already been numerous but isolated intuitions, forerunners of psychoanalysis, so many as to lead Carlo Emilio Gadda to suggest that "Freud did not discover anything entirely new, but only ordered, schematized, settled, and reduced into terms a material already known for centuries."[26] Gadda's suggestion was a certainty for Thomas Mann, who in his lecture "Freud and the Future" (1936) showed that the use of disease (especially mental disease) as an indispensable instrument of knowledge was an idea common to great writers and philosophers of the nineteenth century, such as Novalis, Nietzsche, Sören Kierkegaard, and Schopenhauer (not to mention his precise references to Richard Wagner and Feodor Dostoevski).[27]

More recently Lancelot L. Whyte has systematically examined *The Unconscious before Freud*, analyzing how from 1680 to 1880 human thought established the idea of the existence of the unconscious mind and how the structure of the mind has been explored, especially in our century. After noting that in the idea of the unconcious mind at least three groups of elements converge (*a.* German *Naturphilosophie*, romanticism, and scientific individual psychol-

[25] Michel David, *La psicoanalisi nella cultura italiana*, in particular pp. 18–23. For some contemporary developments, one should remember Ervin Goffman's *Asylums: Essays on the Social Situation of Mental Patients and Other Inmates* and *Stigma: Notes on the Management of Spoiled Identity*; Franco Basaglia's *L'istituzione negata* and *La maggioranza deviante*; and *La fabbrica della follia*, ed. Associazione per la lotta contro le malattie mentali. It is well known that in Soviet Russia insane asylums are used as instruments of political repression against dissenting intellectuals.

[26] Carlo Emilio Gadda, "Psicanalisi e letteratura," in *I viaggi la morte*, p. 48.

[27] Thomas Mann, "Freud and the Future," in *Essays*, pp. 303–324. On the forerunners of psychoanalysis, see also Lionel Trilling, "Freud and Literature," in *The Liberal Imagination*, now in *Psychoanalysis and Literature*, ed. Hendrich M. Ruitenbeck, pp. 251–271; Henri F. Ellenberger, *The Discovery of the Unconscious: The History and Evolution of Dynamic Psychiatry* (he emphasizes the importance of Pierre Janet); and Peckham, *The Triumph of Romanticism*, pp. 13–14. Trilling, after recalling the fact that Freud himself stated that "the poets and philosophers" before him "discovered the unconscious," mentions Diderot, Shelley, George Sand, Tieck, and Stendhal among such forerunners (p. 251).

ogy; *b*. biology, vitality, and organicity; *c*. Oriental mystical ideas), Whyte reminds us that the term *unconscious* (*Unbewusstsein*) was invented by Ernst Platner and dates back to 1776, while Hegel, Friedrich Schelling, Schopenhauer, Nietzsche, and Eduard von Hartmann (all of them anticlassical, anti-European, anti-Enlightenment) are undoubtedly Freud's major precursors during the nineteenth century. Nine editions of von Hartmann's treatise on *Philosophie des Unbewussten* (1868) had been published in Germany by 1882.[28]

It seems amply demonstrated then that Freud did not come out of a void but was rather the culmination of a whole trend in the culture of the nineteenth century. At any rate, Freud had the great merit of systematizing the theoretical study of the irrational and its practical utilization for therapeutic purposes by instituting psychoanalysis, a new discipline. Certainly, only with Freud can the dialogue between reason and nonreason really begin again. Psychoanalysis is recognized in its scientific autonomy, social function, and cultural status, all of which are inevitably reflected also in literature.

Paradoxically, literature's appropriation of medical discoveries begins the inner erosion of the solid, positivist world; the diseases described acquire an elusive, suggestive character (although the method of description remains partially realistic and documentary). In fact they express the inner breaking down of one whole *vision du monde* that is to be replaced by another. The world of objects is no longer a datum, a certainty; the world of others is no longer meaningful in itself, in its institutions; in an apparently contradictory but intimately rigorous way, reason now implies nonreason within itself. The absolute of objectivity becomes, by varying degrees, the relative of subjectivity. What comes to the fore is the awareness of the self with all the ambiguities and the anguish inherent in the discovery of how unstable, contradictory, and absurd the relationships of the self to the world of others and of objects can be. Henri Bergson's *Essai sur les données immédiates de la*

[28] L. L. Whyte, *The Unconscious before Freud.*

conscience and Freud's first psychoanalytical writings were published toward the end of the last century, almost at the same time.

In Italian literature these dramatic developments are recorded
and worked out by two writers in particular: Italo Svevo, who proceeds from a quasi-naturalistic attitude in *Una vita* to the much
subtler representation of disease in *Senilità* and then to the complex
and articulated view of *La coscienza di Zeno* in which the free use
of psychoanalysis acquires an exceptional cognitive and literary
value; and Luigi Pirandello, who deliberately uses madness as a
means of expressing his theories (especially in *Uno, nessuno e centomila* and in *Enrico IV*), perhaps by adhering to Émile Durk-
heim's conception of the marginality of disease considered as a
mirror of the writer's own marginality.

Svevo is more rigorous and, in my opinion, more effective than
Pirandello in his use of disease as a metaphor for inner analysis (of
the Freudian type) and as a protest against his society (capitalistic, bourgeois). On the other hand, Pirandello is more openly
polemical than Svevo in acknowledging the sharp juxtaposition ex-
isting between reason and nonreason and in the paradoxical and
ferocious demolition he makes of it, especially through the social
"role" (in Peter Berger's and Thomas Luckmann's sense) and the
"mask" (in Ludwig Binswanger's sense) with their related
problems.

Both of them, Svevo in a polite and subtle way, Pirandello desperately and dramatically, express the dissatisfaction and alienation of modern man. (Perhaps it is not by chance that in Italian a
madman is also called *alienato*.) But, whether the protest is expressed through neurosis or madness, it goes back to that moment of
inner reflection and self-analysis that marks the beginning of the
twentieth century in literature.[29]

---

[29] Cf. Caute, *The Illusion*, pp. 164–200. This is a provocative discussion of alienation as opposed semantically to Hegel's "abstract" that necessitates its dialectical
counterpart, "concrete." According to Renato Barilli, in *La linea Svevo-Pirandello*, the narrative projects of both Svevo and Pirandello "tend toward the total
institution of a new culture . . . which is fundamentally posited *beyond* the bourgeois one" (pp. 13–14).

It is important to note that the contrast between the self and the world is conveyed not only through the imagery of mental diseases; certain traditional illnesses, like tuberculosis, continue to be thought of and used by some writers as revealing symptoms, as symbols of precisely that contrast. A famous case is that of Franz Kafka, about whom Paolo Milano wrote:

> It is well known that Kafka, from the first moment, in his disease saw the physical manifestation of an inner conflict ("my wound, of which the lung's lesion is only a symbol"). He wrote in one of his notebooks: "The world, of which my fiancée is a representative, and my Self shatter my body in an irreconcilable contrast." At one and the same time, sickness excused him from his duties, in which he believed but to which his strength was unequal. Wagenbach reminds us that this psychogenesis of tuberculosis, sounding like a poetical hypothesis in Kafka's time, today is a diagnosed datum accepted by medicine without difficulty for certain cases.[30]

Actually it has been demonstrated that sickness can be associated with the failure of an individual organism to maintain its integration in the social *telos*: there is a high death rate among motherless children; somatic diseases are frequent among those who have had a traumatic break in their social relationships; and in laboratory experiments some animals brought up in isolation are more subject to cancer than others brought up in groups.[31] In any case it is significant that in his works Kafka did not use physical disease to express his *vision du monde*, but rather preferred to employ the inner world of obsession, guilt, and persecution (from *Das Schloss* to *Der Prozess* and *Die Verwandlung*). He lived his epoch with dramatic awareness and showed it through his characters' sick and morbid introspection.

Another contemporary author can be quoted in this connection: Antonin Artaud, who in his letters to Jacques Rivière and in *Le pèse-nerfs* has brought introspection to bear on the very root of thought, on the phenomenon and process of thinking—the birth,

[30] Paolo Milano, "Ritocchi alla vita di Franz Kafka," *L'espresso*, September 15, 1968, p. 19.

[31] Cf. David Bakan, *Disease, Pain and Sacrifice*.

articulation, and manifestation of thought. Here are some examples from his letters to Rivière:

I suffer from a frightening disease of the spirit. My thought abandons me continuously, from the single fact of thinking to the extreme fact of thought's materialization into words.

This constant breaking down of my thought should be attributed . . . to a central giving way of my soul, a sort of essential and at the same time fleeting erosion of thought. . . . There is then something that destroys my thought, something that prevents me from being what I could be, but that leaves me, if I may say so, suspended. Something stealthy that takes away from me the words *I have found*, . . . and that constantly destroys the mass of my thought in its substance.

Similarly, in *Le pèse-nerfs* he writes:

A concordance of words with the moments of my states of mind is lacking. . . . At every stage of the mechanics of my thinking there are holes, stops—try to understand me— . . . a strained becoming fixed, the sclerosis of a certain state. . . . I am the one who best felt the awful losing itself of his language in relation to thought. I have detected the very moment of my thought's most intimate, unsuspectable crumbling.

The nervous itinerary of thought, rather than the spirit that remains intact, is hit and derouted by this crumbling. It is in the body and in the blood that this absence and this standing make themselves particularly felt.[32]

As did Artaud, and actually before him, with the same effectiveness, the Italian Federigo Tozzi expressed the same type of penetrating and disquieting intuition, full of anguishing questions on the process of thought, hallucinations, the subtle and fleeting borderline between reason and madness, between normal and pathological, in his letters to Annalena dated February 1903:

What is this hand that obeys my thought and traces on the paper signs they made me learn? . . . Who am I? What is my thought? And from what does it derive? Will it be able to die like the flesh dies? Or

[32] Antonin Artaud, "Correspondence avec Jacques Rivière" and "Le pèse-nerfs," in *Oeuvres complètes.*

will it merge once again with the infinite force of all the things of the universe, in the form of another phenomenon, which then, in its turn, will transform itself into another, and then into another, in order not to die and to feel forever? And where will the awareness I have of that thought end up? . . .

And now I have something like a dizzy spell. It seems to me that I am being swallowed by the chasm of a precipice, together with the snow that has enshrouded and overwhelmed me completely. I plunge into it without even touching bottom.[33]

It seems almost unnecessary to underline the dramatic quality of this desperate and lucid introspection on the limits of the self, on the limits of the world and society.

This introspection can be seen precisely as a manifestation of the solitude of the individual vis à vis the society and reality in which he happens to live, milieux that at the beginning of the twentieth century are dominated by bourgeois capitalism, with all the cultural and ideological consequences inherent in it, described from opposite viewpoints by such critics as Erich Auerbach and Georg Lukács. According to Auerbach: "In a Europe unsure of itself, overflowing with unsettled ideologies and ways of life, and pregnant with disaster—certain writers distinguished by instinct and insight find a method which dissolves reality into multiple and multivalent reflections of consciousness. . . . But the method is not only a symptom of the confusion and helplessness, not only a mirror of the decline of our world. . . . There is in all these works a certain atmosphere of universal doom, especially in *Ulysses.* . . . There is often something confusing, something hazy about them, something hostile to the reality which they represent."[34] Auerbach's diagnosis is all the more impressive in that it seems to foreshadow what Frank Kermode has recently called "the sense of an ending," a quality that characterizes our Western culture and is to be found in all of our major

[33] Federigo Tozzi's letters are in *Novale.* The translation quoted is from Giose Rimanelli's remarkable essay, "Federigo Tozzi: Misfit and Master," *Italian Quarterly* 14, no. 56 (Spring 1971): 29–76. On Tozzi, see also Giacomo Debenedetti, *Il romanzo del Novecento,* partially translated as "Federigo Tozzi: A Psychological Interpretation," in *From Verismo to Experimentalism,* ed. Sergio Pacifici.

[34] Erich Auerbach, *Mimesis,* p. 487.

writers.[35] As for Lukács, in an essay on the aftermath of naturalism in Germany—an essay containing assertions that are valid for the rest of Europe as well—he points out and explains that "the individual personality, juxtaposed to society, finds only in itself a point of reference for its moral life and decidedly rejects any social criterion of behavior." Therefore, in many literary works "there is the accusation against a society in which and because of which man withers and succumbs; there is a feeling that the authentic man can realize his inner capabilities only against and beyond present society."[36] As Lukács notes in another essay, there is above all an escape into the pathological as "a moral protest against capitalism," a protest that, however, often lacks "a sense of direction" and expresses only "nausea, or discomfort, or longing."[37] The extreme, psychopathological cases to be found in William Faulkner's *The Sound and the Fury* and in Samuel Beckett's *Molloy* seem to be very pertinent examples of such a literary and cultural development.

Along with Federigo Tozzi, two more Italian writers fit well into both Auerbach's and Lukács's diagnoses: Svevo, "judging and destructive poet of the bourgeoisie," who continued what Verga had begun,[38] and Pirandello, demystifying "conscience" of European decadence.[39] Their characters take on a significance that transcends their personal cases by far and that, precisely through the common denominator of disease, can be linked to similar contemporary ex-

[35] Frank Kermode, *The Sense of an Ending*.

[36] Georg Lukács, *Schriften zur Literatursoziologie*, pp. 530 and 532. Cf. also Giorgio Luti, *Italo Svevo e altri saggi sulla letteratura italiana del primo Novecento*.

[37] Georg Lukács, *The Meaning of Contemporary Realism*, pp. 29–30. Lukács's stance should be located in the context of his problematics compared to those of the subjectivist, antienlightenment writers like Kafka or Joyce. For a spirited discussion of the problem of capitalist decadent literature for the Marxist critic, see "Symposium on the Question of Decadence" (featuring Sartre, Fischer, Goldstucker, Kundera), in *Radical Perspective on the Arts*, ed. Lee Baxandall, pp. 225–239.

[38] Eugenio Montale, "Italo Svevo nel centenario della nascita," in *Lettere, con gli scritti di Montale su Svevo*, by Eugenio Montale and Italo Svevo, p. 175.

[39] Carlo Salinari, *Miti e coscienza del decadentismo italiano*, pp. 249–284.

periences of such writers as Thomas Mann (*Der Zauberberg, Buddenbrooks, Der Tod in Venedig*) and Robert Musil (*Der Mann ohne Eigenschaften*), for whom the pathological plays a similar role; they anticipate typical patterns and attitudes to be found today.[40] One thinks of certain works of Jean-Paul Sartre (*La nausée*), Albert Camus (*La peste*), François Mauriac (*Thérèse Desqueyroux*), André Gide (*L'immoraliste, Les faux-monnayeurs*), Jorge Luis Borges (especially "El Sur" in *Ficciones*), Elias Canetti, or Günter Grass (*Die Brechtrommel,* in whose "transcendental dwarfism" there is a deliberate, clearly antinaturalistic attitude toward and use of disease as social protest).[41] One also thinks of similar attitudes to be found in Elio Vittorini (*Conversazione in Sicilia*), Cesare Pavese (especially the diary and *Il diavolo sulle colline*), Alberto Moravia (from *La disubbidienza* to *La noia*), Dino Buzzati (*Sette piani, Un caso clinico*), Giorgio Bassani (*La lunga notte del '43*), Mario Soldati (*Le due città*), P. P. Pasolini (*Una vita violenta*), Italo Calvino (especially *La giornata di uno scrutatore*), and Gianna Manzini (*La Sparviera*).[42] Even at the level of today's popular literature, as in the case of the Anglo-Saxon horror novel,

[40] A brief treatment of the problem as it occurs in German literature is in *Thomas Mann's Novel Der Zauberberg: A Study* by Hermann J. Weigand; useful remarks on the moral implications of Mann's conception of disease are in an article by the British physician Oliver Jelly, "Fiction and Illness," *A Review of English Literature* 3, no. 1 (January 1962): 80–89. Cf. also Alberto Asor Rosa, *Thomas Mann o dell'ambiguità borghese*, especially pp. 29–30, 101–107, and 147–149.

[41] Cf. Heller, *The Artist's Journey*, p. 116: "A latter-day Hegel would certainly not be at a loss to think of latter-day names to demonstrate the negativity of the spirit of art in its estrangement from the realities of the age; he would only have to recite the names of Baudelaire, Proust, Picasso, Rilke, Joyce, T. S. Eliot, Kafka, Thomas Mann, Sartre, Camus, Brecht; and he might even mercifully suppress those of the minor manufacturers of last tapes, end games, tin drums, rhinoceroses, and other zoo stories about the desolation of the Spirit in the face of a desolate world." A much more positive evaluation of Grass's "transcendental dwarfism" is in Renato Barilli's *La barriera del naturalismo*, pp. 261–268.

[42] Disease as a theme of social protest in an ironical key can be found at the beginning of this century in a rare text by Guido Gozzano, "Guerra di spettri," now edited by Franco Contorbia in *Il lettore di provincia* 3 (December 1970): 14–24.

the psychopathological has become common and is often posited as "metaphor of the a-normalization of daily experience"; through the device of the diaristic form, "the psychopathic character becomes Everyman—the ironic-tragic sign of a universal condition."[43]

In an example taken from Italian literature, Vittorini used disease in a clearly planned and symbolic way as a necessary stage of the "return to man" and the assertion of his dignity by Silvestro in *Conversazione in Sicilia.* "I knew all this, and more besides. I could understand the misery of a sick member of the human race of toilers, and of his family around him. Does not every man know it? Cannot every man understand it? Every man is ill once, half-way through his life, and knows this stranger that is the sickness inside him, knows his own helplessness against it. Thus every man can understand his fellow."[44]

Or, in another example, involving the most typically literary aspects of bourgeois society, Calvino noted apropos of his novel *Il visconte dimezzato,* "For me the leprous have come to mean the hedonism, irresponsibility, happy decadence, the nexus aestheticism-disease, in a certain way the artistic and literary decadence of today, but of all times as well (e.g., the Arcadia)."[45]

Even in the narrative work of a great critic like Edmund Wilson (one remembers especially his psychoanalytic study *The Wound and the Bow*), the metaphoric value of disease stands out as clear and deliberate. In "The Princess with the Golden Hair," according to the rendering by Paolo Milano of the Italian translation,

Imogene confesses her secret to her lover; in fact she shows it to him: a metal corset, with which the lady protects herself from a disease of the spinal column, an ailment that the man will soon discover to be wholly imaginary. Imogene's invisible lesion, her erotic caution, slowly crystallize into a symbol, an "objective correlative" of an imaginary invalid, a secretly guilty rich America. But the blennorrhea with which the courageous but unlucky Ann infects her finally loving partner is the

[43] Mario Materassi, "Il pipistrello nel frigorifero," *Il Ponte* 28, nos. 4–5 (April–May 1972): 650–664.

[44] Elio Vittorini, *Conversation in Sicily,* pp. 87–88.

[45] Italo Calvino, "Introduzione," in *I nostri antenati,* p. xiii.

mark of the poor and oppressed America, bearer of something so strong and instinctive as to outlive any offense.[46]

But, going back to Italian literature, we see that in Svevo and Pirandello disease is also, perhaps, something more than a metaphor. It becomes an existential condition, a true ontological category (of an ontology always historicized). That is why their influence on contemporary writing is so effective and lasting. It would be impossible to review all of today's novels and short stories dealing with diseases, especially mental diseases, which seem to have been multiplied by the Italian economic boom during the past fifteen years. By applying the notion of "pitiatism" to the contemporary situation,[47] one may note that neuroses appear to be a direct consequence of an affluent society, while such traditional illnesses as malaria and tuberculosis progressively disappear from the literary scene as they diminish, obviously, in social reality. Therefore, the writers who are most attentive to the phenomena of their time continue to use disease as a critical, cognitive instrument by applying it to social and cultural circumstances, first at a representative (or naturalistic) level and also at the levels of metaphor (as a social protest) and ontology.

For instance, one thinks of Giuseppe Berto's *Il male oscuro*, which is so far the most immediate and faithful rendering of a psychoanalytical experience in literary form (although this novel, as such, retains perhaps too much of its autobiographical origin), or of the novel-documentary *Angelo a capofitto* by Franco Fornari, the scholar who is well known for his essays on individual and generalized situations of violence, especially atomic war. Other examples that come to mind are *Le libere donne di Magliano* and *Per le antiche scale*, novels set in insane asylums by the writer-physician Mario Tobino; *Cancer oecumenicus* by Mario Miccinesi, with the emblematic title; and *Il gioco e il massacro* by Ennio Flaiano, with its equally emblematic transformations.

---

[46] Paolo Milano, "Opere d'immaginazione di un grande critico," *L'espresso*, August 16, 1970, p. 19.

[47] Debenedetti, *Il romanzo del Novecento*, p. 471.

Then there is the long gallery of novels with more or less neurotic protagonists: the "methereopatic" ones *à la* Musil in Giuseppe Cassieri's *Andare a Liverpool* and in Sandro De Feo's *I cattivi pensieri*; or the clearly representative one (in a social sense) of Alcide Paolini's *Lezione di tiro*; or the narrators in Gianni Celati's *Comiche* and in Sebastiano Vassalli's *Tempo di màssacro*, where neurosis is revealed also through stylistic tics; or the lucid mythomaniacs in Luigi Malerba's *Il serpente* and *Salto mortale*, in Enzo Siciliano's *Dietro di me*, and in Aldo Rosselli's *Professione: Mitomane*. In particular, one should remember Mario Spinella's *Sorella H, libera nos*, where all the levels of neurosis can be traced, from the existential to the social, from the literary to the ontological; Torino Guerra's *L'equilibrio* and *L'uomo parallelo*, dealing with the difficult problem of how to maintain a mental equilibrium and how not to succumb to one's double; and, to name the latest specimens of the series, Ottiero Ottieri's *Campo di concentrazione*, with its deliberately ambiguous title, and J. Rodolfo Wilcock's *Lo stereoscopio dei solitari*, with the almost necessary reference to Borges.

The most interesting and meaningful case among those just mentioned seems to be that of Tonino Guerra, who is Michelangelo Antonioni's screenplay writer, because he makes evident the fact that the theme examined so far is not strictly a literary one, but also one that has invaded other forms of art more immediately expressive than literature, like the cinema. Besides *Diario di una schizofrenica* directed by the poet Nelo Risi, we shall mention only the neurotic heroine in Antonioni's *Deserto rosso*; the mad hero of Carel Reisz's *Morgan*, a movie with the appropriate subtitle "A Suitable Case for Treatment"; the psychopathic girl in Roman Polanski's *Repulsion*; the depressed maniac in Liliana Cavani's *L'ospite*; the young epileptic in Marco Bellocchio's *I pugni in tasca*; and the paralytic nephew in Salvatore Samperi's *Grazie, zia*. Referring to the latter two movies, Moravia wrote, "Risking a symbolic interpretation of epilepsy and paralysis, it could be said that they represent the obsession of today's youth with social and cultural integration, conceived of as an infection; that is, the obsession of feeling sick with the same sickness against which one revolts."[48] Moravia's assertion seems to transcend by far the strictly cinematographic context and to apply to the characters of many contemporary novels. Among them the best results at the artistic level seem to have been achieved by Paolo Volponi (*Memoriale, La macchina mondiale*) and Carlo Emilio Gadda (especially *La cognizione del dolore*), whose characters are animated by an attitude of protest revealing itself first and foremost as disease.

Volponi and Gadda, then, appear significant precisely because they view as privileged the condition of illness—the former portrays disease in the context of an industrial setting and of theoretical utopian reflections; the latter portrays it with a geographic and sociological invention that points to a well-defined reality and culminates in a metaphysical climate. Therefore, they exemplify the present-day interest in everything abnormal and confirm the continuing validity of Auerbach's and Lukács's remarks about the beginning of the century. They also confirm the truth of some of Foucault's conclusions:

There is a lot of talk about contemporary madness, linked with the universe of machines and the waning of direct, affective relationships among men. . . . In fact, when man remains a stranger to the facts of his language, when he cannot recognize any human and living meaning in the products of his activity, when he is limited by economic and social determinations without being allowed to find his homeland in this world—then he lives in a culture that makes a pathologic form like schizophrenia possible; stranger in a real world, he is sent back to a "private world," which no longer can guarantee any objectivity; at

[48] Alberto Moravia, "Il seduttore gioca con la morte," *L'espresso*, May 5, 1968, p. 22; also, in the same article he writes: "Is disease, by creating diversity and modifying one's relation to the world, at the origin of an attitude of revolt? Or is the attitude of revolt, when it becomes impotent, the one that provokes disease? I believe in the former hypothesis. But with one correction. Disease and revolt are the same thing seen according to two different types of optics; for the 'righteous' man, revolt is disease; for the rebellious, disease is revolt. In any case, a serious and lasting revolt (like a poetic vocation) usually has its roots in childhood; therefore, it easily becomes a second nature. So that, reasonably enough, it can be said that one is born a rebel as another is born a poet."

the same time, subjected to the limitations of this real world, he feels it as a destiny.[49]

Disease, far from being a simple aspect of reality, is an integral element of a given historical and social structure taken into consideration by literature; therefore, disease often becomes a point of view, an instrument of knowledge and of totalizing judgment for an author.

But, what is disease for a literary critic? Preliminarily, at a superficial but nevertheless meaningful level, it is easy to note that even the language of criticism has been influenced by medical terminology, as if to emphasize the definitive and metaphoric value of the word, which establishes unsuspected relationships between seemingly distant disciplines. Some examples of terms being used currently are *diagnosis, symptom, prognosis,* the already classic *"referto"* introduced by Gianfranco Contini, *anatomy,* as in Ezio Raimondi's *Anatomie secentesche* and Northrop Frye's *Anatomy of Criticism* (although Frye is reviving an older, genre use of the term), and *physiology,* as in Albert Thibaudet's *Physiologie de la critique* or in Mario Untersteiner's *La fisiologia del mito.* In this connection, the following passage by Heller on Nietzsche is a beautiful example of contemporary critical prose: "Thinking and writing to the very edge of insanity, and with some of his last pages even going over it, he read and interpreted the temperatures of his own mind; but by doing so, he has drawn the fever-chart of an epoch. Indeed, much of his work reads like the self-diagnosis of a desperate physician who, suffering the disease on our behalf, comes to prescribe as a cure that we should form a new idea of health, and live by it."[50] Heller's critical language adheres so closely to his subject matter that one does not know which to admire more, his metaphors or his insight.

Another beautiful example is the following passage by Armando Gnisci: "There is a point where the text reveals itself as incomplete

[49] Foucault, *Maladie mentale et psychologie,* p. 100. This argument finds its amplest polemical thrust in Ronald D. Laing's work, especially *The Politics of Experience* and *Self and Others.*

[50] Heller, *The Artist's Journey,* p. 175.

and requires an intervention. It is the point when the reader discovers that the work betrays itself as a fiction of an illusion, as writing and *récit*, and then it flees from itself or doubles back on itself and is thematized. At this moment the critical space is opened, where another text is introduced like a surgical instrument into the wound of the primary text to extract its 'meaning.' "[51] The medical metaphor used by Gnisci apropos the critical and literary texts seems to indicate a level that deeply surpasses language in its most common usage and to point out fundamental, hidden possibilities.

At this further level, it is also true that, on the one hand, critics like Foucault and Jean Starobinski have devoted volumes to the cultural status, meaning, and history of medicine, while, on the other hand, physicians like Pedro Laín Entralgo and Juan Rof Carballo have been concerned respectively with the relationships between "disease and biography"[52] and between "medicine and creative activity."[53] A scientist like Ludwig Binswanger has examined "the problem of self-realization in art" and that of the artistic, literary, and clinical status of mannerism (a "form of failed existence"), and Jacques Lacan and Sergio Piro have brought their attention to bear upon the language of the unconscious and schizophrenia.[54] Thus one observes a useful interchange between fields of study, including working methods and critical categories and concepts; the point of convergence is structuralism. A very pertinent

[51] Armando Gnisci, *Scrittura e struttura*, p. 49.

[52] Pedro Laín Entralgo, "Enfermedad y biografía," in *La empresa de ser hombre*, pp. 223–255. This source also contains provocative discussions of Unamuno's *La novela de don Sandalio, jugador de ajedrez* (p. 239) and Karl Jaspers's *Allgemeine Psychopathologie* (p. 253). The relationship between biography and criticism is examined by Sergio Pautasso in "Biografia come critica," in *Le frontiere della critica*, pp. 146–155.

[53] Juan Rof Carballo, *Medicina y actividad creadora*. This source also has important pages on poetical and scientific language (chap. 2), medicine, man, and society (chap. 11), and José Ortega y Gasset's *Las dos grandes metaforas* (passim). Cf. also Elizabeth Sewell, *The Orphic Voice: Poetry and Natural History*.

[54] Ludwig Binswanger, *Grundformen und Erkenntnis menschlichen Daseins*, *Heinrich Ibsen und das Problem der Selbstrealisation in der Kunst*, *Drei Formen Missglückten Daseins*, and *Schizophrenie*; Jacques Lacan, *Ecrits*; and Sergio Piro, *Il linguaggio schizofrenico*.

example is found in the following remarks by Umberto Eco concerning Lacan's Unconscious-*Autre*: "The Other . . . speaks in the same way as the poetic discourse does according to Jakobson, through a succession of *metaphors* and *metonymies*. A symptom, which substitutes one symbol for another and makes the process of displacement obscure, is precisely a metaphor; while desire, which focuses on a substitutive object and makes the ultimate aim of any expectation undecipherable, is a metonymy. Because of this aim, every desire, through a chain of metonymic shifts, reveals itself as a desire for the Other."[55] With this example we are well inside the most striking phenomenon of contemporary criticism: psychoanalytic terms, patterns, and methods are taken up and applied in the literary field.

Freud's writings on art have remained exemplary of their kind. In them Freud has clearly formulated some fundamental propositions: the language of a work of art (*Gradiva*'s text or Leonardo's paintings) is the sublimation of given impulses that are repressed or not satisfied in life, and it is, therefore, at one and the same time symptom and cure—an ambivalence that gives rise to a significant chain. The psychoanalyst (the critic) must unwind this chain. Furthermore, Freud instituted fundamental parallelisms between the interpretation of dreams and that of poetry and, in another field, between primitive mentality and neurosis.

Perhaps the best assessment of Freud's limits and contributions to date is Lionel Trilling's "Freud and Literature." Trilling arrives at the conclusion that Freud "finds in human pride the ultimate cause of human wretchedness, and he takes pleasure in knowing that his ideas stand with those of Copernicus and Darwin in making pride more difficult to maintain"; but Freud's man has nonetheless a great dignity, which begins with the recognition that he is "an inextricable tangle of culture and biology."[56]

---

[55] Umberto Eco, *La struttura assente: Introduzione alla ricerca semiologica*, p. 330; also Guy Rosolato, "Etude des perversions sexuelles à partir du fétichisme," in *Le désir et la perversion*, pp. 7–52, speaks of a metaphoric-metonymic oscillation.

[56] Trilling, *The Liberal Imagination*, p. 270. In *Il tè del cappellaio matto*, Pietro Citati defines Freud as "a master of formal analysis" (pp. 143–147).

As Mario Lavagetto recently wrote, "Dr. Freud found himself caught between science and literature," with an "invincible nostalgia" for physiology and biology and an equally invincible attraction and innate inclination toward the written word. Equating science with objectivity and literature with subjectivity, he concludes that "the psychoanalytic paradox consists precisely of the systematic utilization of subjective totality."[57]

I am not pretending to fix the landmarks of psychoanalytic criticism, but since Freud's first writings the contributions on and analyses of famous or less well known texts have increased in a crescendo remarkable for the quantity and subtlety of results. These results have been particular and concrete. Sometimes they concern the interpretation or deciphering of single works or authors—such as Ernest Jones's perhaps too famous *Hamlet and Oedipus*, Marie Bonaparte's *Edgar Allan Poe*, Walter Benjamin's definition of Proust's style as "asthmatic," Michel Butor's *Baudelaire*, Sartre's *Flaubert*, Michel David's "Manzoni e il fiore del male," Giacomo Debenedetti's "Presagi del Verga," and Dominique Fernandez's *L'échec de Pavese*. On the other hand, there have been methodological results, especially in Charles Mauron's "psychocritique," Gaston Bachelard's phenomenology of the imagination, and Sartre's existential psychoanalysis, and one should not forget the psychoanalytical implications of René Girard's *La violence et le sacré*. These results have established the psychoanalytic instrument alongside the traditional ones of literary criticism, from linguistics to stylistics, from symbology to structuralism.[58] In taking stock of contemporary psychoanalytic criticism, David recently re-

[57] Mario Lavagetto, "Il dottor Freud fra scienza e letteratura," *Paragone* 21, no. 246 (August 1970): 44–85. Starobinski, in *La relation critique*, wrote of Freud that "his apparent contempt for art would be nothing else than a defense mechanism destined to mask his 'literary complex' linked with the very origins of psychoanalysis" (pp. 274–275).

[58] Maria Corti and Cesare Segre (eds.), *I metodi attuali della critica in Italia*. See the following essays and related bibliographies: David, "La critica psicanalitica," pp. 115–132; and Raimondi, "La critica simbolica," pp. 69–95. The latter is now available in English: "Symbolic Criticism," in *Velocities of Change: Critical Essays from MLN*, edited by Richard A. Macksey, pp. 118–137.

marked: "The ideal would be that a sound philologist and stylistic critic coexist within the same person together with an experienced psychoanalyst."[59]

Freud's studies on primitive mentality were taken up and developed in a completely different direction by Carl Gustav Jung, who, following a teleologic (not etiologic) conception of disease, often appears, in Debenedetti's words, as "a mystic of illness," "the ally of artists, perhaps their accomplice."[60] Jung in his turn influenced literary criticism with his work on the collective unconscious, the myths and archetypes of mankind. Jung gave impetus to a whole trend of ethnographic and anthropological research (Carl Kerenyi, Mircea Eliade) from which mythologic-symbolic criticism took inspiration. In Italy this type of criticism has only recently been developed successfully, mainly through Ezio Raimondi's teaching and work (and the particular contributions by Furio Jesi on Pavese, Emerico Giachery on Verga and D'Annunzio, and Edoardo Sanguineti on Vittorini).[61]

On the other hand, Freud's studies on the ambiguity of the written word have been explicitly taken up by Jacques Derrida: his "Freud et la scène de l'écriture" is the basis for research that, while being juxtaposed to the ontological structuralism of the other great Freudian, Jacques Lacan, is also perhaps the richest in suggestions and developments for a reexamination of the idea of literature, and particularly for the theme of disease.[62]

There are signs today that Freudian psychoanalysis is felt to be inadequate to deal with the complexities of the contemporary world and does not provide a satisfactory explanation of the nature of art and its relation to society; witness the importance attained by modern biology (Jacques Monod's *Le hasard et la*

---

[59] David, "La critica psicanalitica," p. 120.

[60] Debenedetti, *Il romanzo del Novecento*, pp. 467–468.

[61] Remembering that the developments mentioned in the text mainly occurred after 1966, the reader will find it useful to see David's *La psicoanalisi nella cultura italiana* (especially pp. 323–325) on Debenedetti's Jungism: he was a precursor even in this field.

[62] Jacques Derrida, "Freud et la scène de l'écriture," in *L'écriture et la différence*. Cf., also, his *De la grammatologie*.

nécessité) and anthropology (from Claude Lévi-Strauss to Edmund Leach to Victor Turner and to Girard's *La violence et le sacré*). Within psychoanalytic criticism, in particular, Gilles Deleuze's and Félix Guattari's *L'Anti-Oedipe: Capitalisme et schizophrénie* is perhaps the latest and most extreme example of the "beyond Freud" perspective. They acknowledge the insufficiency of the concept of individual personality and propose that this concept be completely destroyed. "Schizo-analysis" should take the place of psychoanalysis and help us fight the evils of capitalistic society; the unconscious should be conceived of as "non-figurative and non-symbolic, . . . abstract, in the way abstract painting might conceive it."[63]

On the other hand, Morse Peckham's *Man's Rage for Chaos: Biology, Behavior, and the Arts* is perhaps the most interesting example of the "aside from Freud" perspective. His biological and behavioristic approach deliberately does away with any psychoanalytic explanation of the artistic phenomenon; art is part of man's biological adaptation to the environment.[64]

It seems clear that our argument so far concerns a field that is at the same time wider and less specialized than medicine and psychoanalysis considered in themselves. This argument starts with the acknowledgment that disease in general has literary autonomy, which manifests itself first as a theme and as such has a status and meanings that are decidedly its own. For instance, the thematic-symbolic analysis of "literary" diseases is justified and functional in that through it, diachronically, one can obtain an exact *aperçu* of a culture, I should say verified in vitro; thus, through a series of what Cesare Segre called *cronòtopi*, [65] it is possible to outline the historic

[63] Gilles Deleuze and Félix Guattari, *L'Anti-Oedipe: Capitalisme et schizophrénie*.

[64] Morse Peckham, *Man's Rage for Chaos: Biology, Behavior, and the Arts*; cf. also Guido Almansi, "La bassa voglia: Divagazioni sulla 'volgarità' dell'arte," *Il Ponte* 27, no. 4 (April 1971): 491–503, now in *L'estetica dell'osceno*, pp. 195–211; and Giorgio Bàrberi Squarotti, "Stile impulso biologico inconscio," in *Il codice di Babele*, pp. 65–92.

[65] Cesare Segre, *I segni e la critica: Fra strutturalismo e semiologia*, p. 28. A *cronòtopos* is a work of art considered not only in the three traditional di-

development from romanticism to positivism, or from positivism to decadence, with scientific and at the same time textual precision.

On the other hand, the theme of disease, even if considered with all of its implications, may not be sufficient to provide the framework of an analysis encompassing all the major themes of a given writer synchronically examined. In this case the theme of disease can be privileged above the others and become in a way only a pretext for a total comprehension, without losing anything of its specific and autonomous importance. In other words the critic can perform the same selective operation on the writer that the latter performed on reality in the first place.

This is the point where structural thematic criticism comes closest to symbolic criticism. Disease is indeed considered as a metaphor for our time, and the critic must study the terms, the movement, and the meaning of this metaphor inside any literary structure, defining not only its semantic and stylistic characteristics, but also the historical, sociological, existential, and ontological ones. Here, "metaphor and history" (according to Ezio Raimondi's title, beautiful in its juxtaposition of seemingly unrelated terms)[66] really converge, or constitute the dialectical poles on which the progress of culture is articulated. Metaphor (the text, the author) is linked with history (the event, the reader) through an uninterrupted series of codes—in this connection a certain line of Russian formalism, from Mikhail Bakhtin to Jurij Lotman, should be remembered, not to mention Roman Jakobson's statement that a metaphor is destined, in time, to become a metonymy.

Furthermore, and perhaps above all, disease is a metaphor for literature. At this level, explored by Derrida with disquieting insight, the theme of disease can undergo the most unthought-of and stimulating developments because it becomes grafted onto the ancient dispute about the art-sickness relationship and opens up new, vertiginous perspectives.[67]

---

mensions of Euclidean geometry, but also in a fourth one—time, history—taken from the theory of relativity through a structuralist approach.

[66] Ezio Raimondi, *Metafora e storia: Studi su Dante e Petrarca.*

[67] Among contemporary Italian writers, the art-sickness relation is felt tragi-

In his search for the *trace* and *différance*, in his pursuit of the elusive nature of human language and *écriture*, Derrida made a fruitful visit to "Plato's Pharmacy."[68] In an ancient Egyptian legend analyzed by Plato, Thot, the god of writing, is also the master of numbers, calculus, the calendar, funeral rites, and death: "The god of writing therefore is the god of medicine as well. Of medicine: a science and at the same time a hidden drug. Of remedy and poison. The god of writing is the god of *pharmakon*."[69] Presented as a gift to Ra-the-Speaking-God, writing can only be considered as contrary to life, a *pharmakon* that does nothing but displace and maybe irritate pain; therefore, writing is a supplement (or displacement) that, as such, contains a "fateful impulse toward redoubling,"[70] that is, toward *dissémination*.

Derrida then goes on in his development of the chain of meanings implicit within the ambivalent nature of *écriture*, passing from the word in the Greek *polis* to writing as error, from "pharmakos" as scapegoat to the death of Socrates, from the figure of Socrates the Father to Plato's "parricide" word, from cosmos to cosmetics, from *mimesis* to play. All these concepts and themes seem self-generating in a complex system of semantic, structural, and symbolic associations, and all are to be found in contemporary literature and criticism. We should not forget that in his work Derrida comes back *à rebours* from Plato to Jean-Jacques Rousseau to Ferdinand de Saussure to Lévi-Strauss; thus, he is concerned with structural linguistics and anthropology, today's typical "sciences of man."[71] His

---

cally by Cesare Pavese, as can be seen from *Selected Letters* and *The Burning Brand*.

[68] Jacques Derrida, "La pharmacie de Platon," *Tel Quel* 32 and 33 (1968), now in *La dissémination*, pp. 69–197.

[69] Derrida, "La pharmacie de Platon," *Tel Quel* 32 (1968): 28.

[70] Walter Benjamin, "The Task of the Translator," in *Illuminations*, pp. 78–79. He speaks hypothetically of a "pure language," of which both the original and the translation would be but "fragments" and therefore "supplements."

[71] See Richard Macksey and Eugenio Donato (eds.), *The Languages of Criticism and the Sciences of Man: The Structuralist Controversy*; and the essay on Derrida by Paul De Man, "The Rhetoric of Blindness: Jacques Derrida's Reading of Rousseau," in *Blindness and Insight: Essays in the Rhetoric of Contemporary Criticism*, pp. 102–141.

purpose, in Alexander Gelley's words, is to define accurately "the boundaries of an epoch, to define the cultural enclosure (*clôture*) in such a way that its limits are both acknowledged and breached. . . . Derrida does seek to reveal as explicit structure what has generally been an unacknowledged or surreptitious devaluation of the textual."[72] In doing so, he makes a further fascinating contribution to what Ernst Curtius called "the symbolism of the book," by proposing an "open" alternative *à la* Borges.[73]

Significantly, Ezio Raimondi refers precisely to Borges, this "fantastic architect of Babel's library," in giving a teleology to the "bibliographic ritual" inherent in his critical method; if "every book one happens to read, whether great or small, puts back into discussion some elements of one's own mental library," then "actually he who accumulates references and lateral observations seconds not only an instinct of information, but also a more secret line of disquiet, of curiosity ever turning upon itself and almost aspiring to its own transcendence. He acts like the collector about whom Benjamin wrote, whose search is dialectically guided by the double calling of order and chaos, of tactics and adventure."[74]

The theme of disease seems particularly fitting for verifying Raimondi's and Derrida's methods of literary analysis and their results, precisely because it goes to the very roots of the literary fact and has an inherent polysemy. But it is important to keep in mind an essential difference between Raimondi and Derrida. The latter is exclusively concerned with literature; society has disappeared almost completely from his critical horizon. The former, on the contrary, begins with literature (rhetorics, style) but is also interested in history (erudition, philology), and from history he is led to a concern for society. For Raimondi, literature and criticism are clearly valid insofar as they strike a rapport with the society and

---

[72] Alexander Gelley, "Form as Force," *Diacritics* 2, no. 1 (Spring 1972): 9–13.

[73] Ernst Robert Curtius, *European Literature and the Latin Middle Ages*. It is also interesting that Foucault recalls Borges; in the introduction to *The Order of Things*, he quotes the "Chinese encyclopaedia" of which Borges speaks in *Otras inquisiciones* as the element that puts our whole culture in question (p. xv).

[74] Ezio Raimondi, *Metafora e storia*, pp. x–xii.

the history around them, insofar as they are able to mirror and to be mirrored by political-cultural events. In this connection it seems significant to note that Raimondi's latest book, dealing with Bolognese humanists and Renaissance and, in particular, Machiavelli's theater, is entitled *Politica e commedia*, confirming the previous *Metafora e storia* in a more "public" context.[75] Unlike Derrida, Raimondi is the latest representative of a tradition that can be considered as beginning with Giambattista Vico (where one finds not only concern for the word as symbol, but also an interest in language as activity) and continuing with Francesco De Sanctis (with his constant relating of literature to society and history) and Benedetto Croce (who was not only the aesthetician of intuition, but also and perhaps above all a liberal historian). Raimondi is fully aware of the problems of literature in contemporary industrial society, and his rigorous work reflects the image of a critic who is at the same time a citizen.

The following essays deal with some great Italian writers of the late nineteenth and twentieth centuries who were selected at least in part as specimens. Verga, for instance, can certainly be seen as a figure who epitomizes the transition (not necessarily a chronological one) between romanticism, *Scapigliatura*, and positivism, but it is hoped that he will appear also, or perhaps above all, in his individuality, in his "Verghianity," so to speak. Because it is based on specimens, this book is not intended to be a history of modern and contemporary Italian literature, not even so far as the novel is concerned; but I hope it will demonstrate its validity (of method and results) by giving an explanation (synchronically and diachronically) of the major points of this history.

Some provisional or momentarily definitive conclusions (as Eugenio Montale and Musil would say) should be clear by now. On the intertextual level, an analysis of the theme of disease allows a consideration of Italian literature differing in many respects from the more conventional approaches by periods or "isms," especially because through this theme one can focus on "tradition" as much as

---

[75] Ezio Raimondi, *Politica e commedia: Dal Beroaldo al Machiavelli.*

on "the individual talent" (to quote T. S. Eliot). Thus the theory of the impersonality of literature can be put to a test in the close reading and analysis of literary texts.

On the contextual level, an analysis of the theme of disease is a valid instrument for tracing the very precise emergence and development of social consciousness in Italian literature, along with the related problem of marginality, from the individualistic death of Narcisa Valderi described by the early Verga to the preindustrial bourgeois society surrounding Gesualdo and witnessing his hopeless struggle with cancer; from Svevo's smiling and pensive irony in dealing with Zeno's neuroses in a well-established and commercial milieu to Pirandello's indictment of that milieu through Moscarda's "mad" rebellion and to Gadda's inquiry into the modes of identity in a technological society, an inquiry coupled with the anguishing memories of a recent Fascist past and a painful uncertainty about the future.

The third conclusion is consonant with the nature of the methodology adopted to interpret the texts and of the texts used to test that methodology: this book has no conclusion, partly because it is designed to be open (a scholar of Mann or James Joyce or Pavese could easily add his chapter to the ones present) and partly because it has to be open if one is to believe in the symbolism of the book and in the unending pursuit of some truth. In this connection, it might be proper to recall also Leo Bersani's "esthetic of incompleteness," which "is equivalent to an ethic of incompleteness for a self too open to be defined—and confined—by the fixed design of a permanent identity."[76] David Caute's comments about art can be applied to criticism as well: "The struggle against social alienation (*Entfremdung*) and false consciousness requires an alienated (*Verfremdung*), anti-magical art, a dialectical literature which recognizes its own nature and which is self-conscious, anti-mimetic and self-critical. It never aspires to completion. It knits, unravels, knits . . . It is a process as well as a product. This process is both synchronic and diachronic, both genetic and structural."[77]

[76] Leo Bersani, *Balzac to Beckett*, p. 11.
[77] Caute, *The Illusion*, p. 177.

Through a thematic, symbolic analysis of disease in some texts by Verga, Svevo, Pirandello, and Gadda, it will be possible to reaffirm the cognitive function of criticism and literature, both of which are engaged against death, both of which lean over the abyss of a truth that is no longer (or perhaps has never been) anthropotheological.

2. Narcisa's Poison

The Romantics' beauty was Medusean, imbued with pain, corruption, and death.

Mario Praz, *The Romantic Agony*

By the slow striking of the clock in the sitting room of the pleasant country house where the two youths lived, it was a morning hour. Narcisa, white with her delicate waxen paleness, her eyes sparkling with an unusual brightness, flashing with happiness, was sitting with abandon on a sofa beside Pietro.

She was dressed in white, her favorite color, even though it was somewhat late in the season; her hair was gathered softly into a silken net, curling on her forehead almost down to her brows in that daring fashion which recalled the most beautiful heads of Greek statues. Her lovely arms wrapped around his neck, her eyes fastened eagerly on his, she listened to his words, seeming to find pleasure in the clear and perfumed atmosphere created by a thousand sensations of the moment.

This is the opening scene of the ninth and last chapter of *Una peccatrice*, Verga's novel published in 1866, an early work that according to Cattaneo "could have represented the breviary of a young decadent, anticipating D'Annunzio's *Il piacere* by twenty-five years."[1]

The scene presents us with the two protagonists of the novel: Narcisa Valderi, Countess of Prato, and Pietro Brusio, a young bourgeois from Catania, author of a successful play that Narcisa in-

---

[1] Giulio Cattaneo, *Giovanni Verga*, p. 60. The initial passage is in Giovanni Verga, *Una peccatrice e altri romanzi*, pp. 120–121. The following quotations are taken from this edition, and page numbers are given in parentheses in the text.

spired. Given the atmosphere, the feminine hairstyle and trappings (similar to those of the lady from Padua in Ugo Foscolo's *Le ultime lettere di Jacopo Ortis*), and the furniture, this love scene might seem to be a literary equivalent of a painting by Jacques Louis David or a sculpture by Antonio Canova. But, when we examine the scene more closely, it becomes passionate rather than loving, romantic rather than neoclassical, tense rather than calm and composed. In fact, despite the modifiers "softly" and "with abandon," and despite the description of Narcisa's "delicate waxen paleness" and of her beautiful arms wrapped around Pietro's neck, two additional details are striking for the subtle tension they create: Narcisa is portrayed with "her eyes sparkling with an *unusual* brightness, flashing with happiness," "her eyes fastened *eagerly* on his"; also the suggestion that a "thousand sensations" created the atmosphere warns us that we are not dealing with a simple love, but with a great, an extraordinary love, a terrible and fatal passion. Indeed, "never had the beloved woman started with such love into the arms of her lover; never had the siren surrendered more softly, more languidly; never had the sorceress had a gaze more intoxicating, which made the deepest fibers of his heart oscillate convulsively. It seemed that something more than mortal stimulated in her all the most exquisite resources, the most fervent inspirations of the fascinating woman, herself so inebriated by the voluptuousness that she inspired, that she sought to fashion with it an irresistible, a devouring fascination" (p. 121). In this crescendo, stressed by "never," Narcisa appears more and more in her role of *femme fatale*: "siren," "sorceress," "intoxicating," "fascinating," "inebriated," "irresistible," "devouring." These appellations and adjectives had already appeared in the novel, along with others of their kind, such as "sylph," "enchantress," "sultana," "virgin," "swan," "fairy." Here they culminate in the expression "that made the deepest fibers of his heart oscillate convulsively"—one of those expressions that must have contributed much to Luigi Russo's opinion that *Una peccatrice* is "a real museum of romantic horrors, collected and preserved with fearless poor taste, by a bright provincial."[2]

---

[2] Luigi Russo, *Giovanni Verga*, p. 35.

Narcisa turns out to be a *femme fatale* worthy to appear in that other more famous museum, *La carne, la morte e il diavolo nella letteratura romantica,* by Mario Praz. Her beauty is the more fascinating because it is artificial, the more powerful in its consequences because it is fragile in its premises. Let us listen to a confession made by Pietro Brusio:

> I could never explain to you the effect this beauty has on me. It is such that it seems almost a miracle, since it has nothing to justify it. In it everything seems to form a whole of grace and charm; it is a beauty that needs all the resources of make-up, all the seductions of manners and accent, all the charm of the glance and the smile to surround itself with this transparent—indeed illusory, I admit—mist that makes it beautiful, that makes it adorable, so that it seems to be visible only in a cloud, through incense and tinsel. It is a beauty that wants to be so, despite nature that created her plain: she is a plastic figure that has, I would say, only the elements of becoming beautiful and the creative spirit to give birth to all the graces with which it surrounds itself. She faces the mirror as a woman and turns away as a sylph . . . an enchantress . . . a siren. (p. 23)[3]

It is as if Beauty, as a romantic ideal, were reaffirmed despite Pietro's deep consciousness of its frailness, and this frailness in turn forms a further incentive to passion. In this way is born a true faith or religion of love (note: "miracle," "incense," "creative spirit") in which the young Verga undoubtedly shares. Russo characterizes it in very significant terms: "It was a demonic religion; that is, a religion with an anthropolatric setting, in which a mortal creature becomes deified; around her are grouped all the problems of life, from the problem of God to that of the fatherland and of society. Woman becomes a kind of pythoness of a new religion of human passions. . . . It was the religion of the new century, one without God and yet in search of Him."[4] Certainly, in the novel

[3] See Gaetano Mariani, *Storia della Scapigliatura,* p. 588: Narcisa's clothes, "like those of other women in Verga's novels of those years, are minutely described, with a taste already resembling D'Annunzio's."

[4] Russo, *Verga,* pp. 131 and 134; but "Verga's artistic and moral development is centered on the polemic and slow breaking down of this romantic faith in love" (p. 136).

as a whole Narcisa is truly the center, the core of Pietro's life; without her, Pietro is nothing; but Narcisa too is nothing because like him she is a mortal creature in search of a God.[5] In this way the relationship is based entirely on a destructive passion. This helps explain the profound resonance of the name Narcisa: "what a beautiful psychoanalytic name," wrote David recently, after Debenedetti had explained how Narcisa for Pietro represented everything that he was not, exciting in him an "irresistible need for compensation," even for the "redeeming of the ego," not only that of the individual, but also the "collective, provincial, insular" one.[6] Her name is "Narcisa" because she is in love with herself and her own beauty and because she is the mirror of another who would like to, but cannot, recognize himself in her. (Luigi Gualdo wrote a short story entitled "Narcisa" in 1868, and later Camillo Boito took up the theme again in *Senso*, creating in the character of the countess Livia Serpieri "a cursed creature," "the blindly passionate, mephistophelian, and refined priestess of her beauty," according to Gaetano Mariani, and a woman "corroded by a moral disease," in Bassani's words.)[7]

In the whole novel passion is, on the one hand, the object of a subtle and insistent psychophysical analysis, and, on the other hand, it is extremely mythicized. Here is an example of Pietro's lovesickness (he is an unknown provincial youth, repelled by a scornful word from Narcisa): "He got up, slowly, as if his legs were giving way under him, feeling the perspiration freezing on his forehead, his teeth chattering convulsively. By day the count would

[5] On p. 88 of this novel Pietro, turning to Narcisa, says, "You are my God! And I will never have the strength to love you as I would!!!"; Gianluigi Berardi (in "Mito dei primitivi e coerenza storica in *Tigre Reale*," *Studi letterari per il 2500 anniversario della nascita di Carlo Goldoni*, pp. 342–383) finely notes that in *Una peccatrice* "the thirst for love possession" has a "cognitive" aspect and leads to "the discovery of nothingness" (p. 356).

[6] Michel David, *Letteratura e psicanalisi*, p. 157; and Giacomo Debenedetti, "Presagi del Verga," in *Saggi critici, terza serie*, pp. 215–231, quotations on pp. 221–223.

[7] Mariani, *Storia della Scapigliatura*, p. 585; and Giorgio Bassani, *Le parole preparate*.

have been terrified by the paleness and alterations in Pietro's features and by the sinister brightness in his burning eyes" (p. 50).

On the other hand, we remember the scene in which Narcisa, having left her husband, goes unexpectedly to see Pietro, who is now the acclaimed author of a play, and confesses her love to him:

Sometimes when I think about this love, so passionate and so immense, a love I would not have known how to imagine had I not inspired it, I, who have smiled and behaved foolishly amid the even more foolish protestations of a thousand gallants, I, who was stunned by this incense of flattery and suit that the most elegant, the most rich and noble men crowd to burn at my feet . . . I feel a movement of uncertain terror; . . . it seems that this passion must be terrible, devouring, when it reaches such a degree; . . . I think that it must absorb life in a kiss of fire . . . but in a kiss of such ecstasy as to make life seem too small a recompense and the days too short to poison yourself with it . . . (p. 87)

Now the scene is repeated, with Pietro on his knees before Narcisa "as if he had wanted to adore her"; and she asks him "Play for me the waltz . . . 'The Kiss' . . . make me happy" (p. 122).

With Luigi Arditi's waltz "The Kiss" (to which we could ideally add the painting *The Kiss* by Francesco Hayez), our museum of romantic horrors is enriched by another valuable piece. But it is just this waltz that marks the rhythm of the continuation of the scene—a rhythm of Love and Death. Narcisa commits suicide, just as Clary does in Verga's first unpublished novel *Amore e Patria*. Clary, a heroine who is called "the serpent with the face of an angel," poisons herself, dying in front of her lover.[8] In a similar manner, Narcisa takes a lethal dose of opium because Pietro no longer loves her with his former exalting and exclusive love. She will die in his arms, like a Violetta or a *dame aux camélias*, wasted away by consumption and love. Both women are romantic heroines, victims of passion.[9] Precisely in reference to similar heroines,

---

[8] See Federico De Roberto, *Casa Verga e altri saggi verghiani*, pp. 98–99.

[9] The comparison with Violetta is made by Debenedetti ("Presagi del Verga," p. 219), that with the *dame aux camélias* by Russo (*Verga*, p. 35) and Berardi ("Mito dei primitivi," p. 344); Carmelo Musumarra—in *Verga minore*, pp. 50–51—emphasizes the novel's "melodramatic air" and Verga's citations of "the

we can recall Foucault's words concerning consumption, the most typical romantic illness: "The nineteenth-century man became pulmonary by fulfilling, in that fever that speeds things up and betrays them, his incommunicable secret. That is why his illnesses of the chest are of exactly the same nature as those of love: they are the Passion, the life to which death gives a face that cannot be changed. Death left its old tragic heaven; it has become the lyric center of man, his invisible truth, his visible secret."[10]

Foucault's words are easily adapted to the other characters of Verga's youthful novels: the *capinera* nun, Enrico Lanti, Nata, Adele—who die consumptive, of special consumption-passion that is typically romantic, "a sickness of the soul . . . that ends by destroying the body as well."[11] If the body resists too long, it suffices to introduce a dose of poison that will have the same ultimate function as the illness.

However, the death of Narcisa is not exactly, or not only, the death of a romantic heroine killed by her great passion. In having Narcisa commit suicide (just as Flaubert had had Emma Bovary do), Verga wanted in a certain sense to kill the romantic hero while from the ashes of that death he was giving birth to the modern, realistic anti-hero. How?

My entire analysis thus far has been conducted with a partiality that is decidedly reproachable but, I think, justified by a need for clarity. The scene from the last chapter of *Una peccatrice* is constructed of superimposed and alternating layers. So far I have examined only the romantic ones and neglected the others, which I shall analyze now. We must not forget that the novel is told by an impersonal narrator who informs us in the prologue that he limits himself to "coordinating the facts," adding to them only his own "uniform coloring, which could be called the varnish of the novel" (p. 13). For the most part, he bases his narrative on letters and "minute and precise" details, given him by a Dr. Raimondo Angio-

---

most passionate melodies by Bellini and Verdi," some of which are from *Ernani*, *La traviata*, and *La sonnambula*.

[10] Michel Foucault, *Naissance de la clinique*, pp. 173–174.

[11] Mariani, *Storia della Scapigliatura*, p. 606.

lini, the fictional filter of the immature "impersonality" of the young Verga, who is still a "romantic" but open to the scientific and cultural developments of positivism, especially through the *Scapigliatura*, as Mariani and Riccardo Scrivano, in differing ways,[12] have pointed out: "No one, besides myself and my friend Brusio, and perhaps he less than myself, will ever be able to come to know by what extraordinary concurrence of circumstances these two beings (Angiolini in his medical capacity used to say *beings*) met and ended up absorbing each other's vitality. They are among those mysteries that seem too concealed but too well traced out in their development to be accidental. They make us guess at what the knife of the anatomist has not been able to find for us in the fibers of the human heart" (p. 11). In these words lies a literary echo of the eagerness for knowledge subtended to the order with which the surgeon Bichat, years earlier, had introduced into medicine, scientific and systematic research in anatomy: "Open up a few cadavres."[13] The writer's cognitive eagerness is actually more complete than that of the doctor, even at the exact moment when he appropriates some of the latter's scientific, positive terminology.

Recalling now the words of Dr. Angiolini, we understand that it is exactly from his medical view that the symptoms of Narcisa's poisoning are mercilessly observed, even when he is not directly called upon stage or when a certain romantic compassion is mingled with a scientifically precise description. Note the adjective "cold" in the following example: "[Pietro Brusio] was silent, surprised, alarmed by the paleness that covered her delicate features, that betrayed some very slight spasmodic contractions. Cold drops of per-

[12] Riccardo Scrivano tends to postpone the influence of *Scapigliatura* on Verga and to limit it to a "tension toward realism," "more as far as contents are concerned than for expressive or artistic factors in general" ("Il Verga tra Scapigliatura e verismo," *Belfagor* 20, no. 6 [November 1965]: 652–663; quoted material is on pp. 658–659).

[13] Foucault, *Naissance de la clinique*, pp. 125–148. Note that when Flaubert describes the arrival of Dr. Larivière in *Madame Bovary*, his portrait begins as follows: "He belonged to the great surgical school derived from Bichat, to a generation of practical philosophers, now extinguished, who loved their art fanatically" (*Oeuvres*, I, 618).

spiration began to form on the edge of the skin at her hairline" (p. 122). Also, Narcisa's eyes were "greatly dilated," "her pupils holding a frightening fixity," "her lips opened panting . . . in the midst of the spasmodic contractions she could not hide," her respiration was a "breathless and suffocated gasp"; once again "her blue, clear, almost phosphorescent pupils were fixed on his face, without seeing, as if searching for him," and "the skin of her face became dry and the veins began to swell with blood" (pp. 122–123).[14]

When the doctor arrives on the scene, he immediately and intuitively understands the situation and records in minute detail the symptoms of opium poisoning: "The pulse was weak, slow, failing; he noted the dry skin, which at certain points on the arms was spotted with small colorless bubbles. Her face was burning and began to turn livid; her eyes were fixed. She made a great effort not to yield to the heaviness of her lids so as to continue to stare at Pietro, although she no longer saw him. He touched deeply the epigastric region and it betrayed a sharp spasm" (p. 124).

Perhaps it is worth recalling here Flaubert's famous description of Emma Bovary's agony as she dies of arsenic poisoning: "Delicately and almost caressing her, he [Charles] passed his hand over her stomach. She let out a sharp cry. He stood back completely terrified.

"Then she began to groan, weakly at first. A great shivering shook her shoulders, and she became paler than the sheet in which were buried her shriveled fingers. Her irregular pulse was almost imperceptible now.

"Drops trickled down her bluish face, which seemed as if frozen in the exhalation of a metallic vapor. Her teeth chattered, her enlarged eyes looked vaguely around her, and she only answered all questions with a nod of the head." And further on, "At once her chest began to gasp rapidly. Her whole tongue came out of her

---

[14] Cf. a description in *Amore e Patria*, quoted by Cattaneo in *Verga*, p. 27: "The young man, though determined, was not able to sustain the effect of those dilated, phosphorescent pupils, whose pupils were shining in the iris of furious passions."

mouth; her eyes rolled and paled like two lamp bulbs that were
going out, making her look already dead, were it not for the terrifying acceleration of her sides, shaken by a furious breath."[15] One
notes the coincidence of the medical language used by Flaubert and
Verga in describing many of the symptoms and manifestations of
poisoning: greatly dilated eyes / enlarged eyes (then: without seeing / looked vaguely); cold drops of perspiration / drops; paleness /
paler; breathless and suffocated gasp / to gasp rapidly, a furious
breath; the pulse was weak, slow, failing / Her irregular pulse was
almost imperceptible now; livid face / bluish face; the epigastric
region / her stomach (then: a sharp spasm / a sharp cry).

This coincidence between the two descriptions is all the more
extraordinary because, although *Madame Bovary* was published in
1856, Verga did not read it until 1873, many years after writing
Una peccatrice. Therefore this coincidence indicates not common
literary sources or influences, but rather a cultural climate common to the epoch of the two authors or, to use Peckham's words, a
"cultural convergence."[16] Of course, this comparison is limited to
the technical, medical aspects of the descriptions. It in no way regards the artistic achievements or the ideological and poetic coherence of the two texts just examined.

As far as *Una peccatrice* is concerned, Verga alternates dense
clinical notations with passionate passages; participating, romantic
narration with impassive and naturalistic description, to use Lukács's terminology as it is taken up again by Romano Luperini concerning *Eros*.[17] Here is an example:

> "Thank you! . . . thank you! . . ." murmured the dying woman with
> an interrupted gasp that her labored breathing suffocated in her throat;

[15] Flaubert, *Oeuvres*, I, 614 and 622–623. Raffaello Ramat compares the sickness of Erminia's son in *Tigre Reale* with that of Mme. Arnoux's son in *Édu-
cation* ("Etica e poesia nei romanzi giovanili del Verga," in *Ragionamenti morali
e letterari*).

[16] See Verga's letter of January 14, 1874, to Luigi Capuana in Nino Cappellani,
Vita di Giovanni Verga, p. 187; and Morse Peckham, *Man's Rage for Chaos*, pp.
11–12.

[17] Romano Luperini, *Pessimismo e verismo in Giovanni Verga*, p. 33.

"thank you! . . . oh! life! . . . Doctor, make me live . . . he loves me! ! . . . I don't want to die! ! !" she finished in a heart-rending tone.

She could utter no more, although she still moved her lips with great difficulty, and a few hoarse and broken sounds escaped from her dry throat.

She remained as if deeply dozing, attacked from time to time by convulsions, revealing a thousand impressions, now delightful, now sad, in the changing expression of her features. Only her eyes with their wide and clear fixity seemed to anticipate death. (p. 127)

The unfailing progression of Narcisa's delirium and coma is recorded by Verga right up to the end: "Pietro still clutched that body, now a corpse by three-fourths, yet still showing its last convulsive movements, its severely strained gasping for breath, the desperate effort of the pupils to see him. . . .

"Her agony was long, painful, terrible. The doctor, with his hands on her chest to count heartbeats, could barely discern the point at which the sleep of poison coincided with the sleep of death" (pp. 127–128). Perhaps it would be appropriate to note here, in addition to the clinical and passionate language, the almost sadomasochistic taste for the macabre (culminating in the clause "he clutched that body, now a corpse by three-fourths") that remains, however, almost always limited and under control in Verga's context and tone.

On the contrary, in the *Scapigliatura* (the attitudes, themes, and images of which hark back to Novalis, Benjamin Constant, and Charles Baudelaire) this macabre taste acquires a very marked character; for instance, it becomes the central subject of the life and work of Igino Ugo Tarchetti, perhaps the most representative writer in the Lombard group.[18]

Following Enrico Ghidetti's studies, it is interesting to note briefly how the taste for the macabre and the morbid is poised in Tarchetti, characteristically, "between naturalism and decadence."[19] He often insists upon making the most "scientific" obser-

---

[18] In this connection, see also Arnaldo Cherubini, "La malattia nella 'Scapigliatura,' " *La Serpe* 15, no. 3 (1966): 129–136; "La malattia nel Verismo italiano: La poesia," *La Serpe* 15, no. 15 (1967): 161–169; and "La malattia nel Verismo italiano: La prosa," *La Serpe* 15, no. 16 (1967): 97–106.

[19] Enrico Ghidetti, *Tarchetti e la Scapigliatura lombarda.*

vations and using them to constitute the basis for a further exploration of exceptional experiences and events. Among Tarchetti's more or less markedly fantastic works, *Lorenzo Alviati, Riccardo Waitzen, Bouvard, Un suicidio all'inglese, Una nobile follia*, and *La lettera U* are particularly meaningful for the theme under examination—from Lorenzo's necrophilia to the last "manuscript of a madman." But above all, *Storia di una gamba*, intended to illustrate "the relationship between animal pathology and the psychological clinic,"[20] provides the reader with an example of Tarchetti's distinguishing element, and at the same time it markedly differentiates him from Verga, where the psychological clinic is practically absent and where animal pathology is seldom, and never per se, insisted upon.

In *Storia di una gamba*, pathology and psychopathology become macabre through the obsessive attraction that the neurotic protagonist feels toward his severed leg. The limb was amputated by a friend whom the protagonist had betrayed. (Thus, the reader suspects the friend of having committed an atrocious vendetta.) The leg was kept in a "small box made of black wood, with glass panels"; it was "a dried leg, without flesh, with the foot, the ankle, and half the thighbone, which, a bit above the knee, appeared to have been broken and splintered" (p. 190). The writer's insistence on macabre details is marked:

I believe that all those who were subjected to such a mutilation must have half-felt what dying is, they must have guessed its secret partially. The amputated leg was lying there, next to me, on the ground. . . . I wanted to touch it, to raise it with my hands . . . What horror! I felt it heavy, cold, flabby, *dead*, above all, dead. How many parts, how many details I had not noticed before, appeared then visible; how many wrinkles, how many creases, how many effects of nerves and muscles! I touched a sinew, and I saw the foot's thumb raise . . . My God! I threw the leg away from me with horror; and immediately afterward I bent over it instinctively, as if it were still mine, as if it could still suffer. (pp. 202–203)

[20] Igino Ugo Tarchetti, *Tutte le opere*, ed. Enrico Ghidetti, II, 189. The following quotations are taken from this edition.

The leg becomes a true objective correlative for the "hypochondriac" protagonist's inclination toward death: "I feel attracted continuously, incessantly toward death; I cannot escape from this attraction a single moment" (p. 217).

It is also worthwhile to examine briefly *Fosca*, a novel that the author defined as "the diagnosis of a sickness" (p. 243) and that is based on his personal experience. In it one finds again the same elements of *Storia di una gamba*, varied but structurally identical.[21] *Fosca*, a sick and sad woman, is juxtaposed to the healthy and happy Clara even in name (dark/ clear); her sickness is "hysteria, a fashionable one for women, a dissolute infirmity that has the double advantage of provoking and justifying" (p. 275). The male protagonist, at first without knowing it, is ill with the same sickness. Tarchetti's taste for the macabre is focused on the figure of Fosca:

She was ugly not so much because of nature's defects or disharmony in her features (which in fact were partially regular), as for an excessive leanness, inconceivable I should say for one who had not seen her, and for the waste caused in her still young person by physical sorrow and diseases. A light effort of imagination could let one descry her skeleton; her cheekbones and temples had a frightening protrusion, the thinness of her neck formed a sharp contrast with the bigness of her head, whose rich volume of black, thick, long hair (such as I never saw in any other woman) increased the disproportion even more. (p. 278)

Fosca is a Prazian figure that Ghidetti places "at the extreme limit between romantic *faisandage* and the deadly *belle dame sans merci*";[22] she is indeed the woman-skeleton, already glimpsed by Tarchetti in the short story "Le leggende del castello nero" and in the poem "Memento!"—the objective correlative of death:

I ran through the doctor's rooms while he was sleeping dressed on the

---

[21] In this connection see a letter by Tarchetti to a friend: "I have a terrible superstition; it seems to me that this woman draws me toward the tomb; it seems that I am seeing the fabulous Death with her scythe and hourglass coming to kill me, to choke me in her cold spires. When her lips touch mine, I feel the germ of phthisis insinuating itself throughout my fibres" (Tarchetti, *Tutte le opere*, II, 239).

[22] Ghidetti, *Tarchetti e la Scapigliatura lombarda*, p. 260.

sofa, and it seemed to me that I saw the frightful image of Fosca re-
produced in and multiplied by his collection of skulls. (p. 324)

One thing above all . . . contributed to increase my sorrow: the fixed, continuous, horrible thought that that woman wanted to drag me to the
tomb along with her. It was evident that she was to die soon. To see
her, already worn out, already a corpse, embrace me, grab me, keep me
tight to her bosom during her crises gave an ever increasing strength
to my frightening fixation. (p. 359)

The importance of these quotations for the theme under examination seems remarkable, especially within the context of the cultural and literary scene of the second half of the nineteenth century.
As Ghidetti points out: "The dominant *motif* of Tarchetti's narrative, the obsessive *motif* of death and survival beyond it, is a progression toward the pathological, which therefore (in a climate of
decadent avant-garde) expresses a radical social protest, the final
result of a 'perverted Rousseauian heritage,' the 'antisociality,' to
use Lukács's formula. In this perspective, Tarchetti's naturalistic
tales and few poems foreshadow *motifs* and discoveries of decadent
literature."[23]

If through Tarchetti and *Scapigliatura* one arrives at D'Annunzio, through them it is also necessary to go back to Verga. In fact,
Mariani has indicated the correspondence between the love scene of
Tarchetti's *Fosca* and that of Verga's *Tigre Reale*, and Gianluigi
Berardi, also in this regard, has referred to the antinomy between
"healthy love" and "ambiguous, pathological attraction," declaring
that in the young Verga "the theme of illness is directly related to
psychological issues between the disturbing and the demonic."[24]

---

[23] Ibid., pp. 273–274. Also: "The evasion from a hypocritical, oppressive order
is realized in the dimension of sickness, which is the inspirational nucleus of the
novel *Fosca*, even though it no longer is the mysterious consumption of E. A.
Poe's women, nor the providential and purifying disease of the *dame aux
camélias*, but the discovery of a new, exceptional way of being on the threshold
of death" (pp. 264–265); and on the following page: "Giorgio, the neurotic who
feels himself dying next to Fosca, is the forerunner of more or less sick and con-
valescent characters, in whose burning imagination and refined senses the il
lusion of an *art d'exception* was present."

[24] Mariani, *Storia della Scapigliatura*, p. 845, note 120; and Berardi, "Mito
dei primitivi," p. 343.

An example of Verga's macabre taste appears in the short story significantly titled "Tentazione!" (1884), the story of a rape and the consequent murder of the victim and mutilation of the corpse.[25] But, without a doubt, Verga knows well how to control himself, as is seen in his description of Narcisa's agony that is observed almost entirely with a medical eye.

Then we must consider the fact that in *Mastro-don Gesualdo* he substitutes real consumption, the "worm that had devoured all the Trao family," an illness that can almost be statistically documented,[26] for the romantic consumption of early novels. Moreover, the Manzonian, punitive, and "providential" plague is succeeded by the Verghian malaria of Nedda and Alfio Mosca and by the cholera that kills La Longa in *I Malavoglia* and creates a setting for so many of the historical pages of *Mastro-don Gesualdo*; above all, we can consider the calm and solemn measure attained by Verga in his description of the agony and death of La Longa, Padron 'Ntoni, and Gesualdo.

Verga needs to mention only a few details in which the tragic quality of the events is concentrated, as for instance the yellow color of La Longa's cholera or the black of her eye bags and lips when she dies—a death concluded in less than one page: "Maruzza was already in bed, and in the dark at that hour her eyes looked as though death had sucked them dry, and her lips were black as coal. . . .

"So they passed the whole night around the bed in which Maruzza lay motionless, until the candle began to flicker and died out too, and the light of dawn came through the window, pale as the dead woman, whose face was consumed and sharp as a knife and

[25] Apropos of this short story, there are fine remarks in Olga Ragusa, *Verga's Milanese Tales*, p. 76. The plot is summed up in three acts of violence, "of which Verga presents the first by a hiatus in the narration, and the other two by a factual and complete exposition of the events."

[26] See Russo's comment: "Don Diego died of consumption, the sickness which in the Sicilian provinces was up to recent times the most frequent, or the one surrounded with mysterious and legendary terror. Therefore it is not *romantic consumption*, such as the one Verga described in his early novels (*Eva, Tigre Reale*, etc.), but rather a homely and genealogical consumption that destroys entire families and draws them to decadence" (*Verga*, p. 265).

whose lips were black."[27] Even more sober is the description of
Padron 'Ntoni's death:

But Master 'Ntoni had gone on a long journey, farther away than
Trieste and Alexandria in Egypt, that journey from which no one ever
returns; . . . and they all felt that they had the old man right before
their eyes, as they'd seen him the last time they'd gone to visit him—in
that huge, ugly room with the beds all lined up in long rows, so many
beds that you had to search to find him. And grandfather was waiting
for them like a soul in purgatory, his eyes fastened on the door, although he could hardly see, . . . and he almost smiled, the smile of those
who no longer smile, or smile for the last time—a smile that remains
stuck in your heart like a knife. And on Monday when the Malavoglia
returned with Alfio Mosca's cart to fetch their grandfather, he was no
longer there.[28]

In contrast the long sickness of Gesualdo is dwelt upon in greater
detail, from the various consultations of physicians to the agony
and desolate death. Here is the diagnosis of his sickness, made "in
proper style" by one of the doctors, don Vincenzo Capra: *"Pylori
cancer*, the *pyrosis* of the Greeks. There were as yet no symptoms
of ulceration; even the adhesion of the tumor to the vital organs was
not certain; but the degeneration of the tissues was already shown
by certain pathological symptoms."[29] In comparison with the diagnosis, which is expressed in scientific and technical language because it is spoken by the physician, the consultations are described
from the point of view of the protagonist, to whom the medical
terminology is leveled and reduced to "nasty outlandish words"
(*certe parolacce turche*; p. 422):

They examined him, they felt him, as if they were handling a child or
a peasant. They showed him to their apprentices as the quack at the
fair shows the cock with horns, or the sheep with two tails, expounding
the case with mysterious words. They hardly answered him, speaking
from their lips, if the poor devil took the liberty of enquiring what dis-

[27] Giovanni Verga, *The House by the Medlar Tree*, trans. Raymond Rosenthal,
p. 184.
    [28] Ibid., pp. 266–267.
    [29] Giovanni Verga, *Mastro-don Gesualdo*, trans. D. H. Lawrence, pp. 426–427.

ease it was he was nursing inside him, as if he had nothing to do with it, nothing to do with his own vitals! And this lot as well had made him buy a whole druggist's shop; mixtures which you counted by the drop, like gold, ointments which you smeared on with a fine brush, and which opened raw places on you, poisons which gave you colic worse than ever, and left the taste of copper in your mouth, baths and sudorifics which left him exhausted, without the strength even to move his head, seeing the shadow of death already spread over everywhere. (p. 438)

What really interests Verga is the psychological attitude of his character: "And he turned his back on them as his father had done, rest his soul. As soon as he was alone he began to moan like an ox, with his nose to the wall" (p. 447). Even in the death scene the clinical details are reduced to the indispensable minimum and are in fact reabsorbed into the counterpoint of the indifferent servant; just as in the death of La Longa, they are smoothed and forgotten by the desolation of dawn:

He lingered for a day or two still, alternating between better and worse. He even seemed to be reviving a little, when all at once, one night, he got rapidly worse. . . . Now he was high and shrill, now he was worse than a deep bass in his snoring. Hardly had the servant closed his eyes than he heard a strange sound that made him jump up in bed; raucous squeakings, like one who was puffing and panting, a sort of rattling that worried you and made your skin creep. . . . Don Gesualdo meanwhile grew calmer, breathing shorter, seized by a tremor, only making a grimace with his mouth from time to time, his eyes always fixed wide open. All at once he went stiff and was quite still. The window began to whiten. The first bells were ringing. In the courtyard horses were heard stamping, and currycombs rattling on the pavement. (pp. 452–453)[30]

In these scenes even the naturalistic interest in the pathological data is used in an extremely sober way; it passes to a lower plane in a participatory and compassionate contemplation of pain and of the

---

[30] Russo comments on the death of Gesualdo: "A more superficial artist than Verga would have described a physical agony; instead Verga deals with a most difficult representation, the only one that matters for the history of our hero, the agony of his will" (*Verga*, p. 271).

solitude of man, of every man.[31] Gesualdo's cancer becomes the objective correlative of Verga's pessimistic *vision du monde*: it is the
"bitter cancer of suffering" (to use D. H. Lawrence's emblematic
words), a cancer that gnaws a whole life away—first, on the historical and social level, because it undermines Gesualdo's struggles
and rise into the upper class, voiding his efforts, achievements, and
expectations; second, on the ontological level, because Gesualdo's
fate is that of every man, no matter where he finds himself on the
social ladder. Verga has used positivistic science—Claude Bernard's
physiology—as an instrument of knowledge that illuminates the individual and the society around him and at the same time raises
them to universal values. The medical datum is first and foremost
what Pirandello called a "word-thing,"[32] but if the "thing" is a
medical or historical fact, the "word" becomes indeed a symbol—
perhaps the most remarkable achievement of the literature of
Italian *verismo*.

From yet another point of view, Russo distinguishes Verga from
the French naturalists in their most exasperated aspects: "He hu-
manized the life of the forsaken, of the brutes, of the vanquished,
creating a tragedy of feeling where the others saw only a clash of
natural forces. Mental positivism tended to see in man's life a
mechanism that operated by the strength and powers of instincts,
hereditary illnesses, physiological idiosyncrasies. Verga forgot the
brutal and coarse formulae of pathology and saw everywhere *life*,
instead of sickness."[33] Russo's words also explain in part the origi-
nality of Verga compared with that of his friend Luigi Capuana, the
Italian naturalist who in many of his works was precisely concerned with the natural mechanism of pathological cases (*Giacinta*,
"Tortura" in *Fumando*) and of physiological idiosyncrasies (*Ri-
brezzo* or *Profumo*). As Carlo Madrignani has shown, Capuana's
interest in these cases and idiosyncrasies was that of the "artist-

---

[31] On Verga's treatment of death throughout *Mastro-don Gesualdo* and more
precisely on the death scenes of don Diego, Bianca Trao, Mastro Nunzio, and
Gesualdo, there are many sensitive pages in Russo, *Verga*, pp. 265–272.

[32] Luigi Pirandello, "Giovanni Verga," in *Saggi, poesie, scritti vari*, p. 391.

[33] Russo, *Verga*, pp. 68–69.

scientist" who looks at them as exceptions: "the narrator can re-build *in vitro* an anomalous fact in the spirit of one who feels 'normal.' "[34] Capuana exploited the scientific materialism of his times to the utmost in delineating psychological processes with great finesse and perception, carrying them "even beyond the limits reached by contemporary psychiatry."[35] According to Madrignani, in *Profumo* Capuana used contemporary neurophysiology so sharply that he could be considered a forerunner of Freud—a re-markable feat indeed, which Verga could not equal.[36]

But Capuana failed where Verga succeeded, that is, in giving a social dimension to his individual characters, in building a criticism of the society around those who remain cases. In fact, Madrignani says, Capuana maintained a "conservative optimism" typical of "positivistic bourgeoisie's ideology, based on the conservation of the natural and social order, on the belief that everything can be brought back into the confines of general utility."[37] Witness the happy ending and the figure of Dr. Mola in *Profumo*, who is more a confessor than a physician, embodying a conception of moral rather than pure science:

In this perspective, Capuana's psychopathology has only an instrumental meaning: it is used to emphasize the fundamental sanity of man, which is confirmed precisely through the terrible exceptions he analyzes. The task of the artist-psychologist is to make Good prevail, to rationalize the irrational, to bring it back into the confines of bourgeois *vision du monde*, to cover the "monstrosities" perceived by the scientist's eye be-hind philosophic and social mystifications with the veil of universal and eternal values—those of universal "sanity" precisely.[38]

This ideological limitation becomes even clearer in Capuana's subsequent work, especially *Il marchese di Roccaverdina*, with its

[34] Carlo Madrignani, *Capuana e il naturalismo*, p. 168.

[35] Ibid., p. 259.

[36] Ibid., pp. 263–264; cf. also Maria Luisa Astaldi, *Nascita e vicende del ro-manzo italiano*, p. 85; Capuana's treatment of the "complex of the mother" in *Profumo* is considered as a true psychoanalytical process *ante litteram*.

[37] Madrignani, *Capuana e il naturalismo*, p. 272.

[38] Ibid., p. 274.

trend toward spiritualism in the treatment of psychological processes—a trend that will culminate, in much the same way, in Antonio Fogazzaro. Nothing like that in Verga, as we have seen. If
anything, it is Evil which triumphs over Good, cancer over health,
pessimism over optimism. In fact, to go back to an earlier observation: from the death of Narcisa is born the modern anti-hero,
Pietro Brusio, the first of the vanquished.[39]

Even stylistically, the separation between the passionate and
precise prose of the scene of love and death, and the counterpoint-
ing in a minor tone of its sarcastic conclusion, could not be more
marked: "Pietro remained dazed, like a madman; for an entire
month.

"The second month he saw his mother; then his friends. A year
later he reappeared in society. . . .

"His splendid promising talent, which a day's love had elevated
to genius in his ardent soul, had failed with this very love. Pietro
Brusio was less than a mediocrity, dragging out his life in his home
town, putting into rhyme some sterile lines for the name days of his
relatives and squandering as happily as possible his scanty
patrimony.

"Mysteries of the heart!" (p. 128). The romantic echo in the
words "genius in his ardent soul" is used by Verga here as a sharp
contrast to "less than a mediocrity"; and the life Pietro is "dragging
out" is described in details that are not very flattering but are suited
to his figure as a "man without qualities." The ending, as emphatic
and exclamatory as it is, picks up once again the theme of "anatomical" knowledge of the human heart that is proclaimed by the
doctor at the beginning of the novel; but the reader cannot help
comparing Brusio's destiny with Verga's, which was also mysterious, inexplicable in its twenty-year "sterile" silence, in its obsessive
care for his "scanty patrimony."

---

[39] Cf. an analogous observation made by Vitilio Masiello, who quotes a critical
definition by Debenedetti: Verga's early heroes are "the pathetic victims of an
idealism without ideals, they are the first incunabula of a European gallery of
inept, 'out of key' characters. . . . The passion for the ideal was automatically

In his fascinating essay on *Una peccatrice* entitled "Presagi del Verga," Debenedetti put forward a psychoanalytic interpretation in which the public repudiation of the novel made by Verga in 1898 ("to exhume similar sins and similar 'Sinners' is a bad trick played on the public and on the author") assumes the weight of a "compulsory gesture" that reveals the value as "horoscope," as "anticipated revelation" of his entire future destiny as contained in the youthful novel.[40] Debenedetti persuasively illustrates how Narcisa takes on the value of a "fetish," and he declares that Verga's other early novels also "were in a certain sense, instrumental symbols, fetishes, for the conquest of success" and means of magically possessing a life of luxury: once he achieved this success and lost his ambition, Verga was to find his ideal, which is "the ideal of the oyster," and, in so doing, he would be saved from his "sin" (but certain mature works and his final silence remain unexplained).[41]

Giachery has recently added a clearly Jungian dimension to Debenedetti's predominantly Freudian interpretation. He suggests that Verga, arriving at the middle of his life around 1879, felt the need for a "phase of meditation, of return to a center," and this was precisely "at the moment in which he reached maturity, accepting *in toto* the laws of life, the inevitable corrosion of the fancies of youth."[42] The return coincides with the discovery of the "different," of the "primordial," as Massimo Bontempelli rightly calls it, "that which, at the base of all stages of history, remains un-

---

degenerating into a fatal *sickness of the ideal*" (*Verga tra ideologia e realtà*, p. 50).

[40] Debenedetti, "Presagi del Verga," p. 218. Verga's "disavowal" appeared in *L'Illustrazione italiana*, 1898, as an "open letter" entitled "A proposito di una ristampa."

[41] Debenedetti, "Presagi del Verga," pp. 225–226.

[42] Emerico Giachery, *Verga e D'Annunzio*, pp. 160–161. Pietro Guarino considers Verga's early novels as an effort to enter united Italy, with the consequent disappointment in the years 1875–1879, the rejection, and the translation of his personal experience into metahistorical and fatalistic terms (Verga's mother died in 1878) in "A proposito della 'conversione' verghiana," *Belfagor* 22, no. 2 (March 1967): 186–194.

changed," "the constant source of the variations that, in following one another, create it."[43] Giachery states that Verga intentionally directed himself toward this unchangeable base, toward this

anthropological dimension whose rhythm is the eternal return in which dominates "the terror of history," as Mircea Eliade has shown. . . . He is driven toward this by the nostalgia for an absolute duration of time, the anguish of corrosive temporality and of history, which is always *also* a painful choice, detachment, sorrow (and it is not really necessary to underline how much it is so in Verga's characters, from Jeli to 'Ntoni). But Verga sees it *only* as suffering and pain, never as positive conquest. . . . It is not easy to explain why Verga has always illustrated only the negative, painful aspects of what could be positive progress. Perhaps we would have to have recourse to interpretative instruments of "deep" psychology.[44]

For his part, briefly and without insisting, Giachery puts forward the suggestion that Verga shares a kind of spiritual "agoraphobia" that, according to the testimonies of the Sicilians Pirandello and Tomasi di Lampedusa, is typically Sicilian. From a different point of view, Luperini, after recognizing Verga's "sense of mistrust and of near extraneousness to history," explains Verga's attitude as he characterizes an episode from *Mastro-don Gesualdo*: "The fact is that when claims cease to be expression of great personalities and therefore no longer form a part of the romantic individualistic ideology—and become the password of an exploited and potentially subversive class, then they cease to interest and impassion the writer. The limit of Verga's antiromanticism (which never succeeds in freeing itself from romantic-bourgeois individualism) and his polemical pessimism against all revolutionaries, join in this case in an ideological closure, in an intellectual narrowness that marks the whole boundary of Verga's realism."[45]

Undoubtedly, on the historical level, Verga loved Italy with the romantic passion of the *Risorgimento*, and this is seen in his very

[43] Massimo Bontempelli, *Introduzioni e discorsi*; and Giachery, *Verga e D'Annunzio*, p. 162.

[44] Giachery, *Verga e D'Annunzio*, pp. 162 and 171.

[45] Luperini, *Pessimismo e verismo*, pp. 7 and 166–167.

first novels (*Amore e Patria, I Carbonari della montagna, Sulle lagune*). But he, like the other writers of his generation, was disappointed in the ideal of unification because of the great practical, positive problems that followed.[46] Verga makes a great page in history, paradoxically, in the very describing of the misoneism of his characters, and yet he does not succeed in finishing *La Duchessa di Leyra*, because he lacks a true interest in historical evocation and a real political engagement. Instead, Federico De Roberto, a man of a younger and less disillusioned generation, wrote *I Vicerè*, the great historical novel that would have been inconceivable without *Mastro-don Gesualdo*. But, even more than he loved the idea of a united Italy, Verga loved Sicily. He loved the island "with the nostalgia of a lost paradise,"[47] because it was his place of origin and his unrealized ideal.

Verga reveals himself a writer of transition, at once romantic and positivistic, escaping the opposing classifications and justifications of many present-day critics.[48] Verga escapes precisely because he never poses problems in political terms, but rather in terms of demystification and of "critical knowledge of reality,"[49] cognitive acts that precede, and are superior to, politics and history. But Verga is rightly subsumed again into history through one of those mysterious paths of which only the great men are aware, because, even though he was an avaricious and conservative landowner, irremediably fascinated by the old aristocratic world, he succeeded in

[46] A review of Verga's progressive disillusionment is in Russo, *Verga*, pp. 208–236, as well as in Guarino, "A proposito della 'conversione' verghiana," and in Pieter De Meijer, "La Sicilia fra mito e storia nei romanzi del Verga," *La Rassegna della letteratura italiana* 67, no. 1 (January–April 1963): 116–123.

[47] De Meijer, "La Sicilia fra mito e storia," p. 117.

[48] Perhaps the most typical example of a substantially unfair critical attitude is that of Elio Vittorini, who speaks of "our *schifosissimo* Verga, the most reactionary among modern writers, who amidst the humble people . . . looks for an archaic persistence, which allows the writer to escape the problems and tasks of the present and to maintain the old form under the aspect of a scientific, humanitarian interest" (*Le due tensioni*, p. 77).

[49] Luperini, *Pessimismo e verismo*, p. 216. Cf. also Vittorio Spinazzola, "Verismo e positivismo artistico," *Belfagor* 25, no. 3 (May 1970): 247–276.

telling the story of the humble Malavoglia and in describing the rise and fall of the bourgeois Mastro-don Gesualdo.

A similar thing occurs on the personal, psychological plane: the 1898 repudiation of *Una peccatrice* seems directed more to the present than to the past, because, if it is true that from Narcisa's ashes is born the modern anti-hero, in another sense, from Narcisa's ashes is once again born, obsessively, the Arab Phoenix of a feminine ideal, one that is also unrealized: Eva, Nata, Velleda, right up to Isabella Trao, the uncompleted Duchess of Leyra, whose secret "strongly tempted the fantasy of the novelist: the secret of that womanliness, of that eternal feminine, the mirage of his burning youthful imagination."[50]

Thus, on one side, Verga demonstrates spiritual "agoraphobia" toward history; on the other, he is almost morbidly fascinated with female figures like Narcisa Valerdi, Piedmontese and aristocratic, who were incarnations of "the movement of life," its elusiveness and obscurity, a frustrated and disillusioned ideal of beauty and glory.[51]

It is difficult to speak of Verga the man, so jealously bashful and protected by his work; we know very little of his private life, even less of his quiet infancy and of his loves as a bachelor.[52] However, there must have been some sort of crack in his life because it is reflected in his work, in the artistic result. On the one hand, we have his success and fame, much less than what Verga perhaps hoped for and diminished by D'Annunzio's contemporary "spectacular crescendo" in such a way that the latter must have remained constantly for him a model of literary and worldly *médiation*: "The dream of the young Verga—literary triumph—was realized fully by the twenty-year-old D'Annunzio. Verga could never equal the success of the protagonist of his first novel, Pietro Brusio, but D'Annunzio knew how to surpass him boldly, passing from the conquest of Rome to that of Naples, Venice, Florence."[53]

[50] Russo, *Verga*, p. 209.

[51] "The Movement of Life in Verga" is the title of an article by S. B. Chandler in *Italica* 35, no. 2 (June 1958): 91–100.

[52] Cattaneo, *Verga*, p. 20.

[53] Ibid., p. 215. D'Annunzio, born in 1863, published *Primo Vere* in 1879, two

On the other hand, if it is true that he always refused to wed and also continued what Cattaneo calls "romantic effusions" to the Countess Dina di Sordevolo until he was over sixty years old, then the conflict between real and ideal was never really resolved in Verga. In this way he reveals his narcissism, if we accept the theory of Denis de Rougemont on love *tout court* as opposed to matrimony in the Western world, a theory that Verga in a certain way had anticipated, illustrating it at length in his early novels.

We can understand his "persistent raids" into the world of luxury,[54] and above all we understand that they represent a continual negation of what should have been his literary "conversion." Therefore the repudiation of *Una peccatrice*, a "compulsory gesture" made by Verga while he was working on *La Duchessa di Leyra*, shows his true objective—which is the unresolved antinomy, the constant relapse into the temptation to describe the elegant world of luxury and success, to seize from it the secret that is on the lips or on the faces of the *femmes fatales* by whose "Medusean beauty" he at last remained literally "petrified." There is a destiny in names: Narcisa and Pietro are really "Verga's omens." Indeed, if I can take up an observation of Debenedetti and insert it in the structure of René Girard's similar argument that is centered on *désir*, I would say that the character of Pietro Brusio, with the mediocrity and silence that are his "novelistic truth," remains to accuse Giovanni Verga of the unresolved part of his "romantic lie." Yet we must observe that the literary characters examined by Girard find their truth (as well as that of their authors: Miguel de Cervantes, Stendhal, Dostoevski) at the end of a long search, at the climax of a cognitive process that in each case constitutes a conversion, while for Pietro Brusio and Verga the matter is not one of conversion but rather one of "omen," of a rending and yet mo-

---

years before *I Malavoglia*, and *Il piacere* in 1889, the same year as *Mastro-don Gesualdo*. In the past century, Verga's two novels never attained the success they deserve: by 1907 *I Malavoglia* had only six editions and *Mastro-don Gesualdo* only five, while *Storia di una capinera* had reached twenty-two and *Eva* thirteen (see Russo, *Verga*, p. 26).

[54] Cattaneo, *Verga*, pp. 305 and 269.

mentaneous illumination, one that does not modify in any deep and permanent way the course of a life or of a style.[55]

At a further level of interpretation, Verga seems to have always clashed with an objective limit on the possibility of knowledge of the "other," as if the "paradigmatic events"[56] of *Una peccatrice* had shown him once and for all the nothingness at the base of love, knowledge, and the ideal. Perhaps this nothingness can explain the unconscious sadomasochistic fury with which Verga bends over the dying Narcisa and describes her terrible agony, minutely, in long "scientific" observations. Perhaps this nothingness can explain the same type of fury no longer directed against a *femme fatale*, but against "the unhappy and persecuted girl,"[57] the *capinera* nun who wastes away in a convent until she dies (not to mention the girl in "Tentazione!").

It is precisely this nun who shows us an unconscious and revealing constant of Verga's imagination: his last great character, never completed, Isabella Trao, Duchess of Leyra, also passes through the constraint of a convent; and like Manzoni's Gertrude,[58] receives there a misguided education that only increases her aristocratic haughtiness, the haughtiness we see in her even before her dying father, Mastro-don Gesualdo:

He took her temples between his hands and lifted her face to read in her eyes whether she would obey him, to make her understand that it

[55] René Girard, *Mensonge romantique et vérité romanesque*, translated as *Deceit, Desire, and the Novel: Self and Other in Literary Structure*.

[56] Berardi, "Mito dei primitivi," p. 372.

[57] Mario Praz, *The Romantic Agony*. It is also interesting to note that, following a remark by Croce, Praz emphasizes Flaubert's "sadistic obsession."

[58] Many critics, and first of all Russo (*Verga*, p. 258), have recalled the "great Manzonian model." In an exemplary essay, "Manzoni e il fiore del male" (in *Letteratura e psicanalisi*, pp. 317–360), David shows the tremendous importance of Gertrude, "a figure of death": he analyzes her presentation and metamorphic development and links her with Cecilia's mother, another feminine figure that, in such a different context, testifies to the extraordinary (unconscious) coherence in Manzoni's imagination. Some of Manzoni's images are clearly taken up by Verga for his women, who are also figures representing a literal or symbolic death: the "swarm" and the "flower" for Isabella, the neoclassical beauty of a "Greek statue" for Narcisa, the "paleness" for both. Are these coincidences

really was important for him, and that he had that secret on his mind. And as he looked at her like that, he seemed to read in her that other secret, that hidden pain there in the depths of his daughter's eyes. And he wanted to say more to her, he wanted to ask her other questions, at that point, to open his heart as if to his confessor, and to read in her own. But she bent her head again as if she had guessed, with the obstinate frown of the Traos between her brows, drawing back, closing inside herself, with her sufferings and her secret. And he felt himself become a Motta again, as she was a Trao, suspicious, hostile, another flesh. He slackened his arms and said no more. (pp. 451–452)

This is one of the best pages of Verga, one in which impending death intensifies incommunicability, solitude, and failure. It portrays a quality of consciousness that is dreadful in its desolate lucidity.[59]

The same thing happened in the last scene of *Una peccatrice*, although with much less critical depth and much less poetic vigor. The comparison should not seem inappropriate. At least one image unites the two texts and acts as a figurative constant: while Narcisa can no longer see and Isabella does not want to see, there is in the early novel a romantic and desperate embrace of the two lovers ("her wrinkled hands groped for his hands, pressing them greedily, with stubborn obstinacy as if afraid to let them escape" [p. 123]; "her hands seemed to him to press more firmly, as if to thank him and not to leave him" [p. 128]). In the mature novel, there is an embrace, no longer romantic, but anxious and very tender, also desperate, of a father and daughter ("He took her temples between his hands. . . . He slackened his arms").

In these unsuccessful embraces, Verga has placed a little of the sorrowful compassion that he reserves almost exclusively for the feminine characters that constitute the sublimation, if not the dia-

---

caused perhaps by deep affinities between the two authors (whose reluctance to describe sexual scenes and whose human reserve are well known), rather than by a conscious literary imitation?

[59] See a remark by Luperini, *Pessimismo e verismo*, p. 153: "In the fact that Isabella is extraneous and unattainable, there is a coherent development of the naturalist theory of the race . . . and of the economic motivation of the 'stuff' which, as Gesualdo perceives, divides the daughter from the father."

lectic contrary, of the *femmes fatales* (from Brusio's mother to La
Longa, from Mena to Diodata, from Adele to Bianca Trao). However, he has, so to speak, taken vengeance in advance for Isabella's
impenetrability by making her "disgraced" by her cousin La Gurna
(a surname that is found, perhaps not by chance, among the ancestors of the author), just as he took vengeance on Narcisa by making her die of love and poison. Both ended in silence, one not completed in her destiny as a character, the other repudiated; and both
remain unattainable, emblematically sealed in this silence.

   Through Narcisa and Isabella it is possible to perceive the extraordinary symbolic force of Verga's work. Narcisa is at the core
of a book that its author wanted erased, forgotten—an early book,
almost at the origin of his later writing. Thus, it is a book that can
be posited as the very presence/absence (in Derrida's terms) from
which the subsequent writing originates. Isabella, on the contrary,
appears at the final edge of a book that its author could not or would
not complete, and her appearance leaves the cycle of the vanquished
unfinished, open, a broken line rather than a circle.

   Perhaps, seen in the light of a symbolic interpretation, Narcisa
and Isabella represent the initial and final points of Verga's effort
to attain impersonality—the aesthetic ideal that aims at the mirrorlike representation of reality, then tends to become a superreality
of style in itself; finally "even the 'reality' of the person who does
the writing becomes a hateful obstacle to the ultimate rational and
aesthetic triumph."[60]

   In cultural terms, Verga's final silence can be taken to represent
the romantic ideal turning into the "craving for nothingness," to
use Nietzsche's words;[61] it was the all-pervading sickness of reality
(Gesualdo's cancer, not Narcisa's poison) that finally gnawed
Verga's page, leaving it forever white and open.

[60] Erich Heller, *The Artist's Journey*, pp. 96–97: significantly, these words
refer to Flaubert.
   [61] Ibid., p. 96.

3. Zeno's Last Bomb

> *And of course we have it now, the sense of an ending.*
> *It has not diminished, and is as endemic to what we*
> *call modernism as apocalyptic utopianism is to politi-*
> *cal revolution.*
>
> Frank Kermode, *The Sense of an Ending*

"To be a healthy man—these words seem to me
to encompass a whole history of happiness!"[1] This
sentence, which seems written by a Svevian character but was instead jotted down by Svevo's younger brother, Elio Schmitz, in his
diary on September 25, 1885, epitomizes the sentiments of all
Svevo's major characters and points to the essence of his *vision du
monde*.

Elio Schmitz suffered from nephritis and died prematurely.
Svevo felt the loss of his brother deeply,[2] and it is fair to say that
Elio's long sickness and death provided the motivating force for his
brother's preoccupation with health. As early as 1884, in reviewing
Émile Zola's *La joie de vivre* for the Triestine paper *L'indipendente*, Svevo wrote, "It seems that Paulina's character is health,
and sickness that of her ancestors."[3] In another article, using language typically half-naturalistic and half-metaphoric, he wrote:
"In the human organism, generally, there is already the germ of
disease. It is a germ that, rationally controlled, produces a virtue;

[1] Gian-Paolo Biasin, "Documenti per Svevo: Dal diario di Elio Schmitz," *MLN*
83, no. 1 (January 1968): 107–125; quoted material is on p. 125. The text of
Elio's diary is now available in *Lettere a Svevo*, ed. Bruno Maier.

[2] Livia Veneziani Svevo, *Vita di mio marito*, p. 18, speaks of Elio's diary,
which "Ettore kept religiously throughout his life, like a precious relic"; and p.
28: "Such a loss left a wake of unforgettable melancholy in Ettore."

[3] Italo Svevo, *Racconti. Saggi. Pagine sparse*, p. 576.

certain special conditions are necessary for it to produce disease."[4]
And reviewing a novel by Jacques Claretie, significantly entitled
La cigarette, he noted: "Nervous finesse is almost never to be found
in a perfectly healthy and robust person, and the saying that gave
our fathers so much confidence and tranquillity, 'Mens sana in
corpore sano,' seems somewhat obsolete."[5] His juxtaposition of nervous finesse and perfect health seems to foreshadow the rivalry between the Svevian protagonists and their antagonists, as well as the
secret superiority of the former.

In the early comedies we find anticipations of attitudes and
themes that will become fundamental for the understanding of
Svevo's whole *oeuvre.* In *Le ire di Giuliano* (1881), Giuliano's
desire for "improving" his own character and "being healed" by
his beloved Lucia is very clear, and this desire is linked to jealousy,[6]
exactly as it is in Svevo's *Diario per la fidanzata* (and later novels):
"January 5, 1896, 11 A.M. . . . I immediately smoked a cigarette to
mark the time and I made the iron deliberation to sacrifice this vice
to you, my Livia. . . . It is a question of loving well and calmly, of
having healthy nerves in order to be healed of the doubts and to feel
love with equal intensity every morning, every evening."[7] In this
and the examples quoted from Svevo's early criticism we see some
evidence of the complex and ambiguous semantic network that
gathers around the idea of disease and spreads into such different
directions as the protagonist-antagonist rivalry or the habit of chain-
smoking and marking time.

But there is yet another area in which disease appears as a central
metaphor, and this area can be identified with the novel *La coscienza di Zeno.* The novel ends with the word *disease:* "There
will be a tremendous explosion, but no one will hear it and the earth
will return to its nebulous state and go wandering through the sky,
free at last from parasites and disease."[8] Zeno's last bomb, his

[4] Ibid., p. 593.
[5] Ibid., p. 620.
[6] Italo Svevo, *Commedie,* p. 34.
[7] Svevo, *Racconti,* p. 769.
[8] Italo Svevo, *Confessions of Zeno,* trans. Beryl De Zoete, p. 398. Numbers in

apocalyptic vision, is linked to Svevo's very early concern with disease, and in fact it appears to be its extreme consequence: in other words, disease seems to be the element that unites Zeno's personal world with the cosmos. Thus, a cosmic explosion is not an absurd ending for a novel of the self (the English translation of the novel's title is significant in its inaccuracy: *Confessions of Zeno*).

Let us see how Svevo dealt with disease in his major novels. In *Una vita* (*A Life*) the sickness and death of Signora Carolina, the mother of the protagonist, Alfonso Nitti, are seen in their most detailed symptoms and manifestations and described in a language that is plainly naturalistic: the inexorable progression of heart disease is shown as an "organic disease," and the author points out the "swelling" and lividness of an "organism in decay," the "cold sweat" and "fast and shallow" breathing, the eyes "shining and dilated with anguish," the "dislocations of the nervous system," and the "bed sores." When Signora Carolina becomes so weak that she is even "incapable of pain," her voice changes, "its tone deeper and less sonorous," and her breathing, already rapid and insufficient, fades to a death rattle (chap. 16, passim). Svevo is fascinated and horrified by the way death takes complete possession of a human organism, but he places such anguishing details in a context quite different from one that a Zola might have provided. These details serve as a counterpoint to Alfonso's thoughts, dreams, and reflections, a counterpoint to his states of consciousness; they underscore his ineptitude and weakness in his intersubjective relationships, especially with the doctor, the tutor-notary, and the servant, but also with some of the villagers; they provide him with a psychological alibi for abandoning Annetta, whom he loves; they provide him with an excuse for self-pity; and they prompt certain generalizations that will become characteristic of Svevo later: Alfonso "felt incapable of living. Certain feelings which he had often tried and failed to understand made life painful and unbearable to him. . . .

parentheses after quotations in the text refer to this edition, as well as to the following: Italo Svevo, *A Life*, trans. Archibald Colquhoun; and Italo Svevo, *As a Man Grows Older*, trans. Beryl De Zoete.

He had to destroy this organism of his which knew no peace" (p. 397).[9] The inner dimension of the naturalistic, medical details is further emphasized by the *malessere* Alfonso feels after seducing Annetta and by his typhoid fever after his mother's death.

Philip N. Furbank argues that "what Svevo is diagnosing in Alfonso, of course, is the *mal du siècle*, which indeed was the reigning idea of the literary period in which he began writing";[10] and he quotes Max Nordau's description of "degenerates" as a particularly fitting one for the protagonist of *Una vita*:

> They have to fight in the struggle for existence, and there is no leisure for them to perish in a slow decay by their own incapacity for work. The normal man, with his clear mind, logical thought, sound judgment and strong will, sees, where the degenerate only gropes; he plans and acts where the latter dozes and dreams; he drives him without effort from all the places where the life-springs of Nature bubble up, and, in possession of all the good things of this earth, he leaves to the impotent degenerate at most the shelter of the hospital, lunatic asylum, and prison, in contemptuous pity.[11]

Along a similar line, Eduardo Saccone concludes that *Una vita* is an "unmasking of Schopenhauerian illusion and romanticism";[12] in fact, the overall atmosphere of the novel is predominantly naturalistic, up to the final letter—a "human document" indeed—with which the Maller Bank announces Alfonso's suicide.

In Svevo's second novel, *Senilità (As a Man Grows Older)*, certain patterns that were noticeable but secondary in *Una vita* reappear in a more complex and subtle structure. The protagonist, Emilio Brentani, is a weak, dreamy, contemplative person who at the age of thirty-five falls in love with Angiolina Zarri, a splendid creature whom Svevo presents as the very portrait of youth and

---

[9] Also, p. 282: "The fact of those healthy and strong organisms being destroyed or created uselessly had given him his first doubts."

[10] Philip N. Furbank, *Italo Svevo: The Man and the Writer*, p. 160.

[11] Ibid., pp. 161–162.

[12] Eduardo Saccone, "*Senilità* di Italo Svevo: Dalla 'impotenza del privato' alla 'ansiosa speranza,' " *MLN* 82, no. 1 (January 1967): 1–55; quoted material is on p. 11.

health—thus contrasting her, structurally and from the outset, with those characters who represent senility and disease:[13]

She was a tall, healthy blonde, with big blue eyes and a supple, graceful body, an expressive face and transparent skin glowing with health. As she walked, she held her head slightly on one side, as if it were weighed down by the mass of golden hair which was braided round it, and she kept looking down at the ground which she tapped at each step with her elegant parasol, as if she hoped there might issue from it some comment on the words that had just been spoken. (p. 3)

Youth incarnate, clothed, would have walked like that in the sunlight. (p. 174)

Yet even Angiolina's character, as well as, somewhat ironically, the idea of health, is treated at one point so as to indicate that the "perfect human health" of which Svevo speaks in *La coscienza di Zeno* is impossible: "She remained thoughtful for a few moments, and then complained that one of her teeth was aching. 'This one,' she said, opening her delicious mouth for him to see, and displaying her red gums and strong white teeth, which seemed like a casket of precious gems chosen and set there by that incomparable artificer— health. He did not laugh, but gravely kissed the mouth she held out to him" (p. 14).[14] Actually, the episode is emblematic of two quite different characters, and Emilio is certainly not the more realistic

---

[13] On the meaning of senility in Svevo's terms, see Russell Pfohl, "Imagery as Disease in *Senilità*," *MLN* 76, no. 2 (February 1961): 143–150. Cf. Furbank, *Italo Svevo*, p. 168: after underscoring "the central analogy between Emilio and Amalia—two dreamers, a day-dreamer and a nocturnal one, a comic and a tragic one, side by side," he continues: "Balli and Angiolina are the representatives of health, Emilio and Amalia of sickness; Balli and Angiolina the embodiments of sunlight as against the shadowy existences of Emilio and his sister." The most sensitive and philosophically complete treatment of the point in question is perhaps to be found in Saccone's article, "*Senilità* di Italo Svevo," p. 8: the characters of the novel are grouped by juxtaposition (Emilio-Balli, Amalia-Angiolina, Emilio-Angiolina) and by correlation (Emilio-Amalia, Angiolina-Balli, Amalia-Balli). The result is a system in which, in Lukács's terms, the "degraded hero" lives in a "constitutive opposition" with the "sufficient community."

[14] Cf. Svevo, "Diario per la fidanzata," in *Racconti*, p. 777: "January 19, 1896. Poem written in bad prose. My spouse is a candy and I hope that my rotten teeth, by eating it, will be healed."

of them: in fact he idealizes Angiolina and calls her Ange (p. 19).
By contrast, Stefano Balli, an energetic, active, determined artist,
who mediates Emilio completely and has all the attitudes of a
"superior person" (p. 65), sees Angiolina in a very earthy, precise
way, and calls her "Giolona, . . . emphasizing the broad vowels to
the utmost, so that the sounds conveyed the maximum of contempt" (pp. 60–61). Emilio, who deceives himself into believing
that he, "a superior being, an immoralist" (p. 18) like Balli, has
corrupted Angiolina, is really unable to cope with a situation of
"triangular desire" (as Girard would put it): "This was perhaps
the cure he had been hoping for. Polluted by the tailor, possessed by
him, *Ange* would soon die, and he would continue to amuse himself
with Giolona; he would be gay, as she wanted all men to be, indifferent and cynical like Balli" (p. 62). The word "cure," in the
preceding passage, is important in that it reflects the key trait of
Emilio, his "disease" as opposed to Angiolina's health, a twist never
mentioned or specified explicitly except in the title of the novel.
The inauthenticity of their relationship is admirably expressed in
the same passage by the absence of their first names and the abun-
dance of conditional tenses.

A fourth character, Amalia—Emilio's sister, weak and dreamy
like her brother, humble and gray—provides another important
dialectical element in the structure of the novel. Together, Amalia
and Emilio embody disease, senility, contemplation, and nonlife,
while Balli and Angiolina embody health, youth, action, and life.
Small wonder that Amalia falls in love with Balli, as Emilio does
with Angiolina; small wonder that Emilio is mediated by Balli and
mediates his conception of Angiolina through the image of Amalia,
his alter ego.[15] In this way, then, the intersubjective relationships

---

[15] Cf. Svevo, *As a Man Grows Older*, p. 244: "Years afterwards . . . Angiolina
underwent a strange metamorphosis in the writer's imagination. She preserved
all of her beauty, but acquired as well all the qualities of Amalia, who died a
second time in her. She grew sad and dispirited, her eye acquired an intellectual
clarity." Also, see the psychoanalytical interpretation by Paula Robinson, "*Senilità*: The Secret of Svevo's Weeping Madonna," *Italian Quarterly* 14, no. 55
(Winter 1971 [1970]): 61–84; and Guido Almansi, "Il tema dell'incesto in Italo
Svevo," *Paragone*, no. 264 (February 1972), pp. 47–60.

in the novel define and control its structure, especially through the significant dichotomy between health and disease and the attention accorded the latter in the narration.

It will be useful at this point to examine the long description of the sickness, agony, and death of Amalia. As in *Una vita*, this description appears naturalistic in its candor concerning the symptoms and in its insistence on painful details, one of which—Amalia's alcoholism—contributes decisively to her decay and death and echoes *L'assommoir* directly. Two whole chapters (12 and 13) are dedicated to her pneumonia. After finding her half-naked on her bed and delirious, Emilio summarizes for the doctor her symptoms, the most interesting of which is her panting. He particularly emphasizes its sound, a circumstance that seems important because something similar, equally powerful, is described in *La coscienza di Zeno*: "He had been listening to it since the morning till it seemed to have become a quality of his own ear, a sound from which he would never again be able to free himself" (pp. 210–211).[16] Amalia's death is then described in a passage dramatically divided into two parts by a chapter heading and similar to one in *Una vita*, but more important; in fact it echoes philosophical positions derived from Schopenhauer and Nietzsche, based on the preeminence of the bodily datum, which will be fully developed in *La coscienza di Zeno*:

[Amalia's deathrattle] was in fact the lament of matter which, already abandoned by the spirit, and beginning to disintegrate, was uttering the sounds it had learned during its long period of painful consciousness.

The image of death is great enough to fill the whole of one's mind. Gigantic forces are fighting together to draw death near and to expel it; every fibre of our being records its presence after having been near

16 And again, p. 233: "Amalia's breathing became more and more rapid, then grew slower and slower, and finally ceased. The interval was so long this time that Emilio cried aloud with fear. The breathing began again, calm for a short time, and suddenly quickening to a dizzy speed. It was a period of agonising suspense for Emilio." Similar situations reappear in *La coscienza di Zeno* with the deaths of Zeno's father and Copler, and are catalyzed in the obsessive image of the panting train engine.

to it, every atom within us repels it in the very act of preserving and producing life. The thought of death is like an attribute of the body, a physical malady. (pp. 237–238)[17]

Despite Svevo's literal description of the effects of disease, in *Senilità* even more than in *Una vita*, sickness and death serve chiefly to counterpoint the protagonist's states of consciousness and, more precisely, to define his sense of guilt toward his sister. Amalia becomes a metaphor for Emilio: her sickness corresponds to his progressive decay, her delirium to his dreams and behavior.[18] Indeed, the whole novel is filled with images and metaphors taken from medical terminology and applied to Emilio's states of consciousness or to Amalia's feelings—"malady," "treatment," "recovery," and the like. Other terms are used to denote physiological reactions to psychic or emotional states: for instance, *malessere* (significantly translated as "prickings of conscience," p. 49), "stomach ache," "indisposition," "paralysis."

Thus disease is no longer merely a naturalistic fact: it reflects the drama of the psyche. Disease becomes literally a metaphor for analysis and introspection. Indeed, Svevo himself seems aware of

---

[17] The last words of the quotation are, in Italian, "una malattia dell'organismo," and are applied by Svevo, later on, to life itself. Marziano Guglielminetti, *Struttura e sintassi del romanzo italiano del primo Novecento*, p. 139, makes perceptive remarks on Schopenhauer and Nietzsche as possible influences on Svevo's language. Cf. also Gennaro Savarese, "Scoperta di Schopenhauer e crisi del naturalismo nel primo Svevo," *La Rassegna della letteratura italiana* 75, no. 3 (September–December 1971): 411–431. One might only add that the "Superman" was seen by Svevo with irony and antipathy, as in the earlier version of the "immoral superior man" embodied in Balli.

[18] The correlation between Amalia and Emilio is emphasized again and again in the novel; see pp. 120, 125 (Amalia is referred to as "this other dreamer"), 130, and 226: "He scrutinized her, he analysed her, so as to be able to feel her sorrow and to suffer with her. Then he looked away again, ashamed of himself; he had become conscious that in his emotion he had gone in search of images and metaphors." One should also notice that in her delirium Amalia invokes Balli, while Emilio dreams of being seriously ill and taken care of by Angiolina (p. 154). But, as Saccone points out (*"Senilità* di Italo Svevo," pp. 31 and 35), notwithstanding these correlations Emilio remains different from and superior to Amalia. Unlike his sister he is problematic and dissatisfied and longs to improve his present reality.

the fact that such a process has been developing in his writing and in his *vision du monde*. He even portrays his protagonist, Emilio Brentani, in the midst of a similar process: "Why revolt against the laws of nature? Angiolina was a lost woman even in her mother's womb. . . . It was useless to punish her: she did not even deserve it: she was only the victim of a universal law. The *naturalist* who somewhere lay hidden in him revived" (p. 97, italics added). "Feeling that speech would betray him in a situation like the present, because of his tendency to analyze everything, he immediately had recourse to what he knew to be a more forcible argument: abandoning her" (p. 99). In Svevo's work this process of metaphorization reaches maturity in *La coscienza di Zeno*, where in fact the circle is closed by the episode in which chemical analysis is juxtaposed with psychoanalysis:

Paoli analyzed my urine in my presence. The mixture turned black and Paoli looked grave. At last I was going to have a true analysis after all this psychoanalysis. . . . Nothing took place in that retort to remind me of my behavior with Dr. S., when, to please him, I invented fresh details of my childhood in order to conform to Sophocles's diagnosis. Here was only the truth. The thing that had to be analyzed was imprisoned in the phial and, incapable of being false to itself, awaited the reagent. When that came it always responded in the same way. In psychoanalysis, on the other hand, neither the same images nor the same words ever repeat themselves. It ought to be called by another name: psychical adventure, perhaps. (p. 378)

Actually, in order to probe Svevo, one need only apply a stethoscope to his life, so to speak, to auscultate his letters and the diary for his fiancée in order to confirm the symptoms observed in his literary works of what disease and recovery, introspection and action, dream and reality meant in his life. Thus he writes to Livia Veneziani on December 23, 1895: "I gave you my first kiss with the same coldness with which I would have signed [*paraphié*] a contract; I gave you the second kiss with the enormous curiosity of analyzing you and me. . . . Now I understand less and less; certainly my capacity for analyzing is much less great than I thought." And on May 26, 1898, "Whereas, when we married, I asked you to dream with me, now I'll ask you to help me remain fixed in real life, with my eyes wide open watching for thieves."[19] Svevo's capacity for analysis was, in Carlo Bo's words, not only "a literary tool," but also "a norm" in his life.[20] And it is accompanied, underscored, and expressed by the typical terminology examined so far. His diary for his fiancée, for instance, is filled with his desire to be "healthy and strong," to have health like his blonde Livia; at the same time, in the same pages, there are the doubts, the anguish, the depressions, the hopes of a man who feels much older and poorer than his woman, a man who is therefore tormented with jealousy (the leitmotiv of Zeno's last cigarette begins also here) and who even writes the "Truthful History of My Probable Recovery."[21]

In *La coscienza di Zeno* disease is both a real and a metaphorical element presiding over the structure of the narration, and it crystallizes into its major components—the psychoanalytical, the sociological, and the ontological.

In saying *psychoanalytical* I am oversimplifying the term. In fact bodily disease is presented throughout the novel in various guises, but virtually all the maladies, illnesses, ailments, *et similia* that torment Zeno are nothing but the raw material for his real disease, which is nervous, psychic, and, to be more precise, psychosomatic; for instance: "I told him [Dr. Paoli] of my insomnia, my chronic bronchitis, the eruptions on my face which were tormenting me just then; of the sharp stabbing pains in my legs, and finally of my inexplicable lapses of memory" (p. 378).

The trend already manifest in the first two novels ultimately found scientific support in the discoveries of Freud, so that after twenty-five years of silence Svevo was able to assert his previous insights with greater authority. Psychoanalysis then provided him

[19] Italo Svevo, *Epistolario*, pp. 40–41 and 115.

[20] Carlo Bo, *L'eredità di Leopardi e altri saggi*, pp. 481–482.

[21] Svevo, "Diario per la fidanzata," in *Racconti*, pp. 765–795, in particular the entries for January 30, February 12 and 13, 1896; see also in *Epistolario* the letter of July 14, 1901, to his wife.

with the link that he had long sought between positivism and subjectivism, between objectivity and relativity.

Yet, as many critics have pointed out,[22] Svevo's attitude toward psychoanalysis was fundamentally ambivalent, perhaps because, in his moderation and critical stance, he could not accept the new medical science as a panacea.

His ambivalence is amply demonstrated from a historical and biographical point of view, and it has its correlative in the structure of *La coscienza di Zeno*, where even the title hints that the character Zeno is not really cured by psychoanalysis but by his own *coscienza*, his awareness of himself, of his own condition of being sick, and of his acceptance of it (as we shall see later).[23]

But for Svevo disease in this novel represents more than a psychosomatic manifestation. Although *La coscienza di Zeno* is constructed around an unusual (i.e., literary) case of psychoanalytical treatment, beginning with the ironic preface by Dr. S. and ending with a chapter on psychoanalysis, it seems clear that what really matters in the narration is the autobiography of the author. Svevo universalizes himself through Zeno while keeping him at a distance by interposing another fictional character who through his assertions makes of Zeno a highly "unreliable narrator," to use Wayne C. Booth's famous term. Dr. S[vevo] is the dialectical opposite of Zeno-Svevo, in a way reminiscent of the literary displacement experienced in Roland Barthes's equation S/Z; he says: "I

[22] Cf. Arcangelo Leone De Castris, *Italo Svevo*, pp. 341–351; Giulio Cattaneo, *Esperienze intellettuali del primo Novecento*, pp. 119–137; Michel David, *La psicoanalisi nella cultura italiana*, pp. 386 and 392–393; André Bouissy, "Les fondaments idéologiques de l'oeuvre d'Italo Svevo," *Revue des études italiennes* 12, nos. 3–4 (1966): 209–245 and 350–373; 13, no. 1 (1967): 23–50; quoted material on p. 368. Also see Furbank, *Italo Svevo*, pp. 175–177; and Eduardo Saccone, "Svevo, Zeno e la psicanalisi," *MLN* 85, no. 1 (January 1970): 67–82.

[23] Giacomo Debenedetti maintains that Svevo failed to "express the Jewish soul" and therefore was not a great, universal writer. See *Saggi critici, nuova serie*, particularly "Svevo e Schmitz," pp. 49–94, written in 1929. This position is hardly acceptable: cf. Furbank, *Italo Svevo*, pp. 98–99. One should also see Debenedetti's *Il romanzo del Novecento*, where this same position is restated on p. 624 after having been practically denied in the preceding pp. 516–616.

must apologize for having persuaded my patient to write his auto-biography. Students of psychoanalysis will turn up their noses at such an unorthodox proceeding. But he was old and I hoped that in the effort of recalling his past he would bring it to life again, and that the writing of his autobiography would be a good preparation for the treatment" (p. 1).[24] So even "autobiography" is not a com-pletely accurate term; it will be noted that in the Italian text Svevo, following the early usage, writes *"psico-analisi"* with a hyphen that cuts the word and seems to underscore (if only because of the accent) *"analisi."* In fact, in *La coscienza di Zeno* his capacity for analyzing the unconscious motivations of men becomes as subtle as possible. But (and here is the point) the character's capacity for analysis is always presented as a symptom or effect of disease and is therefore metaphorical. An example of this is Zeno's statement about his wife, Augusta, who seems to possess "perfect health in a human being," or rather to be actually "personified health": "I am trying to arrive at the source of her well-being, but I know that I cannot succeed, for directly I start analyzing it I seem to turn it into a disease. And now that I have begun writing about it I begin to wonder whether health like hers did not perhaps need some treat-ment or training to correct it" (pp. 142–143). Thus the contem-plative stance of man—his terrifying power to destroy life by means of thought, an idea one finds in Pirandello's *Il fu Mattia Pascal* and *Uno, nessuno e centomila* or in Miguel de Unamuno's *Niebla*—seems to be regarded by Svevo as the only real and incurable condition. Indeed, Zeno's struggles to stop chain-smoking, his "sentiments filiaux d'un parricide" (of a parricide *manqué*, to be sure, and with a complex of guilt), his being me-diated by others, his marriage, and his business partnership—all can be seen, at one level of interpretation, as attempts at self-

[24] Cf. Sigmund Freud, *Therapy and Technique*, p. 125: "It is incorrect to set the patient tasks, such as collecting his memories, thinking over a certain period of his life, and so on." See also Svevo's "Profilo autobiographico," in *Racconti*, p. 807: "It was then [in 1918] that Svevo tried some experiments in psychoanalysis on himself, but in solitude, which is in perfect contradiction with the theory and practice of Freud. The whole technique of the process remained unknown to him—a fact that anybody can realize in reading his novel."

awareness disguised and perfected through a fake, literary psycho-analytic process—in other words, as efforts to be cured, to reach health. But, as John Freccero has remarked, "it is Zeno's intelligence which converts the rhythm of life into disease, by analyzing and dissecting, by searching for stability in the present and substituting self-consciousness for action, chain-smoking for life. . . . The intellectual desire to know liberty leads to the paralysis of discontinuous time—disease, Zeno calls it—whereas the flow and rhythm of animal health preclude the exercise of what is distinctively human—thought."[25]

Such is the predicament, or "disease," of Zeno: to live and at the same time to observe himself living; to be and at the same time to know. This predicament is humorously described in two famous episodes, when Zeno limps on hearing that there are fifty-four movements in the muscles of a moving knee and when he plays the violin while beating the tempo with his foot.[26] As it develops, Zeno's intellectual disease, his absorption by analysis and contemplation, leads him more and more into abstractions, toward the condition of theory, and toward an absolute knowledge of life that can be expressed or represented in very general terms, like those of parables or fables, which indeed are to be found at the end of *La coscienza di Zeno*, as well as in the stories "La novella del buon vecchio e della bella fanciulla," "Una burla riuscita," "La madre," and "Il vecchione." On April 4, 1928, the very old Zeno noted: "I now know that the things I put down were not the most important: they became so, simply because I fixed them with words, and now, what

[25] John Freccero, "Zeno's Last Cigarette," *MLN* 77, no. 1 (January 1962): 3–23, now in *From Verismo to Experimentalism*, ed. Sergio Pacifici, pp. 33–60; quoted material is on pp. 49–51. Cf. also Glauco Cambon, "Zeno come anti-Faust," *Il Verri* 11 (December 1963): 69–76: "Health and disease are then identified with innocence and self-awareness" (p. 75).

[26] Note that in both cases Zeno's failure and disease are closely and inevitably linked with the thought of Ada. Sandro Maxia notes, "The music coming from the world of the healthy has definitely segregated Zeno in his own time, which is different, untimely" (*Lettura di Italo Svevo*, p. 130). As for limping, its symbolic and psychoanalytic aspects are treated in general terms by René Girard in "De l'expérience romanesque au mythe oedipien," *Critique* 222 (November 1965): 899–924.

am I? Not the one who lived, but the one whom I described."[27]
Zeno's predicament could not be stated in clearer terms, his disease
could not be diagnosed more acutely.

Yet, at another level of interpretation, analysis and introspection
can be seen as a manifestation of the solitude and alienation of the
individual within the society in which he lives, so that Zeno's is
actually the typical bourgeois disease, in this case described by
Svevo from within the bourgeoisie.[28] It will be useful to note at this
point that Zeno Cosini as well as Emilio Brentani and Alfonso
Nitti suffer from the same symptoms as does the very first protagonist in a story by Svevo, the poor porter, Giorgio, of "L'assassinio di Via Belpoggio" (1890). Giorgio is called "il signore," and he
commits a murder in order to become a member of the rich bourgeoisie, the "sad society" around him by which he is constantly
mediated, made discontented, and shunted aside.[29] Giorgio needs the
fictional reality of murder so that he can feel inferior, persecuted,
and guilty, and so that he can long to improve himself while being
fearful of being judged by the others—at once analyzing his act and
incapable of living. The murder is a sort of pretext for a fictional
parable that develops Hegel's dialectic of master-slave, as well as
Svevo's own dialectic between contemplation and action, thought
(awareness, *coscienza*) and life.

In the novels that follow, Svevo does not need the metaphor of
murder to portray protagonists with exactly the feelings and attitudes of Giorgio. They will not need to kill in a literal sense in order

[27] Italo Svevo, *Further Confessions of Zeno*, trans. Ben Johnson and P. N.
Furbank, p. 27.

[28] Renata Minerbi Treitel suggests that the etymological meaning of the name
Zeno is "stranger," while the name *Cosini* might point to "reification," with a
clear allusion to contemporary "alienation" ("Zeno Cosini: The Meaning behind
the Name," *Italica* 48, no. 2 [Summer 1971]: 234–245).

[29] Svevo, *Racconti*, p. 226. Critical analyses of "L'assassinio di Via Belpoggio"
are in Eduardo Saccone, "Il primo racconto di Italo Svevo," *Filologia e letteratura*, nos. 45 and 46 (1966), pp. 93–112 and 201–218; and in Savarese, "Scoperta
di Schopenhauer." Now it appears that Svevo's very first story was "Una lotta,"
published under the pseudonym E. Samigli in Trieste's paper *L'indipendente*,
January 6–8, 1888: see Ruggero Rimini, "Un inedito di Svevo," *Belfagor* 26, no.
5 (September 1971): 599–600.

to exist; for them, Giorgio's murder becomes, indeed, a pre-text, one that explains their life and their disease in a powerfully literary and sociological way.[30] In Furbank's words: "The sickness from which the Svevian hero suffers, the total subjectivity and divorce from external reality, is the quintessence of the bourgeois disease, as seen in Marxist terms. Opposites meet; and spiritually Zeno is, if not a born capitalist, at least a born expression of the capitalist ethos. . . . His relation to the things he deals in is purely functional. They, like his mistresses, have no existence except in relation to himself."[31] And Eugenio Montale has called Svevo "the poet of our bourgeoisie—a judging and destructive poet" who continues what Verga began, "the epic of a growing bourgeoisie that is almost nearing its dissolution."[32]

In contemporary Italian literature there is another author who can help to explain Svevo in relation to the metaphorical and sociological function of the pathological: Paolo Volponi. In Volponi's first novel, *Memoriale* (1962), the character Albino Saluggia is shown alone and alienated in today's industrial society. He believes that some physicians have plotted to keep him out of the factory where he belongs; but he is actually sick (tuberculosis), and his persecution complex is clearly a neurosis, straight from the title. By inverting the terms of the situation in which Svevo portrayed Zeno, *malade imaginaire*, Volponi clarifies the structural significance of the pathological, a significance that was perceived in critical (rather than fictional) terms by Auerbach and Lukács.

But the critic must examine further the complex universe of Svevo and pass beyond the sociological and historical levels to the

[30] Cf. Svevo's "Poesie in prosa di Ivan Turgenjeff," in *Racconti*, pp. 572–574; also, the comedy *Inferiorità* (1921) is based on typical ingredients of Svevo's story, such as the ineptitude of the protagonist, the master-slave relation, and the ensuing murder.

[31] Furbank, *Italo Svevo*, pp. 189–190.

[32] Eugenio Montale, "Italo Svevo nel centenario della nascita," in *Lettere, con gli scritti di Montale su Svevo*, p. 175; also cf. Giorgio Luti, *Italo Svevo e altri saggi sulla letteratura italiana del primo Novecento*, pp. 260, 269, 273; Guido Guglielmi, *Letteratura come sistema e come funzione*, pp. 122–123; Alfredo Bonadeo, "Ideale e reale nella *Coscienza di Zeno*," *Italica* 46, no. 4 (Winter 1969): 402–418; and Norbert Jonard, *Italo Svevo et la crise de la bourgeoisie européenne*.

ontological level in his consideration of Svevo's use of disease. To quote Furbank again:

What makes Italo Svevo a major author is the generality and universality of his handling of disease. It should be remembered that the last two decades of the nineteenth century, with their preoccupation with the *mal du siècle*, marked a genuine historic crisis, one out of which psychoanalysis was born. The conviction that something was sick in the whole European society was as authentic as it was ill-defined and superstitious. It was Svevo's importance that he saw the dangers of any such conviction of disease. . . . His own lifework as a writer (and it was especially the task of a comic writer) was to show that if the *mal du siècle* were studied with genuine detachment it revealed itself neither as something to be proud of, as a distinguishing possession, nor ashamed of, as a symptom of degeneracy, but as something familiar and indistinguishable from life itself. It was restored to the order of nature.[33]

The passage from history to ontology is described clearly in the above quotation; and another critic, Sandro Maxia, underscores the same passage very effectively when he states that "the nexus health-disease . . . in Svevo expresses an opposition *inner* to the bourgeois order," recognizes that *La coscienza di Zeno* "develops the nexus health-disease toward the perfect ambivalence of the two terms," and concludes that "the social class and its limitations have ultimately become symbols of an ontological human condition."[34] Let us see, then, how such a passage is articulated by the structure of the novel.

In *La coscienza di Zeno* disease first appears in connection with a *vision du monde* that is historically derived from Schopenhauer and Nietzsche, one that is seen in Svevo's preceding novels; for instance, Zeno says to his newly born nephew: "Poor innocent, you continue to explore your tiny body in search of pleasure; and

[33] Furbank, *Italo Svevo*, p. 190. Interesting considerations on Svevo's "sense of disease" and "love for truth," comparable with Thomas Mann's and Musil's, are in Giulio Cattaneo, *Esperienze intellettuali del primo Novecento*, pp. 122–124 and 128–129. Cf. also Lilian R. Furst, "Italo Svevo's *La coscienza di Zeno* and Thomas Mann's *Der Zauberberg*," *Contemporary Literature* 9, no. 4 (Fall 1968): 492–506.

[34] Maxia, *Lettura di Italo Svevo*, pp. 152 and 175.

the exquisite discoveries you make will bring you in the end disease and suffering, to which those who least wish it will contribute. What can one do? It is impossible to watch over your cradle. Mysterious forces are at work within you, child, strange elements combine. Each passing moment contributes its reagent. Not all those elements can be pure, with such manifold chances of infection" (p. 4). Life as disease is presented here *in nuce*; the equation is developed later in the novel in a longer passage, a passage that could be considered an ironic summa on the subject:

But I alone lived by Basedow! He seemed to me to have penetrated to the roots of life, and shown it to be as follows: all living beings are ranged along a certain line, at one end of which is Basedow's disease. All who are suffering from this disease use up their vital force recklessly in a mad vertiginous rhythm, the heart beating without control. At the other end of the line are those wretched beings, shriveled up by native avarice and doomed to die from a disease that looks like exhaustion but is really cowardice. The happy mean between these two maladies is to be found in the middle of the line, and is called health, though it is really only a suspension of movement. . . . Those at the center have the beginnings of either goiter or dropsy, and all along the line throughout the whole of humanity there is no such thing as perfect health. (pp. 286–287)

To understand Basedow fully, perhaps it will be worth turning to a curious story by Svevo that seems the perfect fictional realization of the main idea outlined above. The story is entitled "Lo specifico del Dottor Menghi," and it is an interesting example of what today would be called science fiction with a philosophical basis.[35] Dr. Menghi discovers a medicine that controls the excess of vital force, so that life can be prolonged indefinitely: "Latent force is the only force; that which we can perceive with our senses or measure with our instruments is the loss of force" (p. 537). This medicine, called Annina after the inventor's mother, is conceived

---

[35] According to Bruno Maier, the story was written at least before 1904, because Svevo mentions "Lo specifico" in a letter to Livia Veneziani of that year: see the introduction to Svevo's *Racconti*, p. 12, note 8. Numbers in parentheses after quotations from this short story in the text refer to this edition.

particularly as "the pharmakon for intellectuals, not for manual workers" (pp. 539–540), because, although it calms down all the senses and slows life itself almost to a standstill (precisely the opposite of Basedow's disease), it leaves the intellect extremely lucid and better able to analyze the senses:

> I did not run toward action and enjoyed the idea that by now I could measure an abyss without jumping into it. . . . Oh, the effect of Annina was beyond any expectation! The effort to perceive an object was largely compensated for by the finesse of the sight. I was able to analyze the slightest nuance of colors. Up to then a gas flame had been yellow with some red reflexes and blue at bottom; stupidly yellow, in sum. Now I saw it was not like that and discovered the most varied gradations of those various colors in the flame. (p. 452)

The trouble is that sentiments and sorrow (the moral conscience) are obscured by Annina, as Dr. Menghi soon finds out after experimenting on himself and even on his dying mother (a fact that is in itself important because of its connection with Zeno's sentiments for and against his father). Actually, the medicine turns out to be "the equivalent of a disease" (pp. 549–550); a small wound is not painful and does not begin to heal as long as the effect of Annina lasts.

The story ends with the triumph (but a risible triumph) of Dr. Clementi, the exuberant antagonist of Dr. Menghi. "Lo specifico del Dottor Menghi" is important and significant for its portrayal of the antithesis between contemplation and action, thought and life, in purely fictional terms through the metaphors of medicine-disease and of life-disease. Its conclusion, "Let's remain mortal and good-hearted" (p. 553), will be fully developed in *La coscienza di Zeno*, as the passage on Basedow shows and as another paragraph at the end of the novel illustrates: "I am not so naïve as to blame the doctor for regarding life itself as a manifestation of disease. Life is a little like disease, with its crises and periods of quiescence, its daily improvements and setbacks. But unlike other diseases life is always mortal. It admits of no cure" (p. 397).

The ontology underlying the idea that life is disease is completed by the consequent idea that real health is actually death. It is well known that Svevo was dominated by the thought of death, and in fact, on the very last page he wrote before dying, we find the passage "The thought of death must be the thought of a healthy man. It must be alive and strong, not sick."[36]

There is a striking similarity between Svevo's conception of life and death and that of Carlo Michelstaedter, a resemblance that is all the more striking because there are no proofs of acquaintance or friendship between the two writers, and consequently the similarity must be ascribed for the major part to a common background of Mitteleuropean culture and sensitivity. Michelstaedter was born in 1887 at Gorizia, a city not far from Trieste, into a bourgeois Jewish family; he committed suicide in 1910 in his home town. He had just graduated from the university of Florence, having written a thesis, *La persuasione e la rettorica*, that deals with the ideas of ancient Greek philosophers like Socrates, Plato, Aristotle, Parmenides, and Heraclitus and that in contemporary terminology could actually be entitled "Authenticity and Inauthenticity"; he also wrote *Il dialogo della salute*, which sums up the themes of the thesis in literary form, and some poems, mostly directed to Senia, his beloved. His life was dominated by his longing for an ideal absolute, a desire that sprang from his study of Schopenhauer and Nietzsche, an active, energetic, youthful *vision du monde*; it ended in death—like a rigorous syllogism. With frightening foresight, Michelstaedter summed up his whole life, past and future, in a short, unobtrusive note written in 1905:

A young man, educated in a religious school, as a reaction to it, turns to anything that appears to be against the human laws and ripens through his speculations on the psyche of man and on the mystery of nature. He sees too much, and in his embittered soul the source of feelings dries up. He feels it and is sorry for it; therefore, he wants to throw himself into life to excite the paralyzed fibers of his soul with strong sensations. And he does so. But he cannot regain the lost spontaneity and realizes that his enthusiasm is fake. . . . With his usual, cruel sin-

[36] Livia Veneziani Svevo, *Vita di mio marito*, p. 156. Now see Mario Fusco, *Italo Svevo: Conscience et réalité* (an ample psychoanalytical and sociological study), especially pp. 291–317.

cerity toward himself, he examines his own interior, analyzes it, and then, with a calm and reasoned resolution, he kills himself, thus giving back to mother earth the energies that were struggling uselessly inside himself.[37]

In Bo's words, Michelstaedter's "total participation" in life (and in death) derived from "the opposition between his own God and the history of men, from the impossibility of finding a compromise between the ideal and reality, between his longing and the mechanical possibilities."[38] Michelstaedter's is a rare example of an uncompromising philosophical attitude, one with a corresponding behavior; his life and his beliefs form a totality that is authentic and tragic.

At the center of Michelstaedter's theory is the "dull, continuous, measured sorrow that imbues all things" (p. 23)—Schopenhauer's universal sorrow—that is to be faced and "lived" by man if he wants to reach his authenticity, his "persuasion." For the common man, this sorrow culminates in the thought of death; since "he who fears death is already dead" (p. 34), Michelstaedter wants to teach men how not to fear death, how to be healthy by making death part of their lives (like the Stoics, or the existentialists):

> Alas, we did not dream of this bitter death
> in its pale frightening aspect,
>
> .   .   .   .
>
> but the young death, smiling
> at him who does not fear it—
> that death which unites
> and does not divide the companions,
> and does not press them with the obscure sorrow.
>
> (p. 403)[39]

[37] Carlo Michelstaedter, *Opere*, p. 630; see also his letters, particularly the last one addressed to his mother on September 10, 1910 (pp. 617–621). Subsequent references in the text are to this edition.

[38] Bo, *L'eredità di Leopardi*, pp. 51–52. Also cf. Antonio Piromalli, "Carlo Michelstaedter, la crisi della persona e della cultura," in *Saggi critici di storia letteraria*, pp. 165–181, especially p. 169.

[39] This is part three of "A Senia," a poem that is beautifully interwoven with images of "the deserted sea," "the savage sea," as a metaphor for an authentic

Not dissimilarly, Svevo left the following note: "A time will come, when man does not fear death."[40] Accordingly, Michelstaedter's energetic pessimism has something in common with Svevo's ironical self-analysis. The connection appears most clearly in *Il dialogo della salute*, an essay that begins in a cemetery with the warden saying to two friends, "May God give you health" and ends thusly:

Health belongs to the man who, in the midst of all things, "consists" [i.e., stands firm]; who lets his needs and hunger flow through himself and "consists"; who . . . has nothing to defend against others and nothing to ask of them, since there is no future for the man who expects nothing. He does not have this or that emotion, this or that feeling— joy, anguish, terror, enthusiasm; but the sorrow of common deficiency talks to him with a unique voice, *and he resists it with his entire life* in each of its points. He looks death straight in the face and gives life to the corpses around him. His firmness is a vertiginous way for the others who are in the stream. Darkness for him is split by a shining wake. This is the lightning that breaks the fog. And death, like life, is without weapons before him—he who does not ask for life and does not fear death. But with words of fog—life, death, more and less, before and afterwards—you cannot talk of him, *who, consisting in the point of health, has lived the beautiful death.* (pp. 365–366)

"To live the beautiful death" is not a paradox, but the completion of an absolute ideal, the culmination of authenticity: like a chrysalis, "with the thread of life" Michelstaedter spun his destiny "toward that death" (p. 369).

Thus the authentic man is healthy; he is one who lives and dies without compromises, who accepts his own being, the world, and others without illusions, without exceptions, without fear. On the contrary, too many men deceive themselves with fake values, with inauthentic beliefs; these men are vain and sick. Michelstaedter describes their mode of being in various fields of human endeavor.

---

life-death. See also the poems "Aprile," "Onda per onda batte sullo scoglio," and "I figli del mare."

[40] Livia Veneziani Svevo, *Vita di mio marito*, pp. 180–181. Such an attitude might be construed as a reflection of Nietzsche's Superman, "the prototype of health" according to Erich Heller, *The Artist's Journey into the Interior*, p. 192.

For instance: "They go on talking and talking and through the 'word' delude themselves into believing that they are asserting their individuality, which escapes them. In fact others want to talk, not to listen: so they murder and contradict one another. They don't care if a thing is said, but each one wants to be the one who said it. Hence the introductory particles of speech have taken up weapons, so to speak, and have become adversative" (p. 343). Language reflects the limitations, the sickness of man; in describing the subjunctive as "the elementary mode of subjective reality," Michelstaedter gives many examples based on the concept that "Whoever reflects is sick" ("È malato chiunque rifletta"), thus emphasizing "the necessity inherent in reflection" (pp. 145–147), just as Svevo does in his polemic against the Subject, *La coscienza di Zeno*.

According to Michelstaedter, those who search for the truth and deceive themselves into believing that knowledge is an absolute value per se are also "outside of life and of health in their organic beings. Betraying nature, which wants persuasion in the complete man, they have betrayed themselves. Their conscience is not a living organism, a presence of things in the actuality of their persons, but a memory . . . and the presence itself of memory next to the actuality of one's own person is a malady: an organic being does not tolerate extraneous bodies" (p. 68). Zeno's painful efforts to recollect his past are a perfect illustration of Michelstaedter's assertion.

Still another consequence of his theory should be stressed, because it is important in connection with what was said earlier about disease and psychoanalysis: "The farther man goes from nature, the more he is impotent, angry (sick). . . . The fact by now is no longer only an individual one, but, by centuries-old movement, atavistic. And complacent science has immediately found a name for this inevitable disease and a right for it to exist in society; every petty act has received its pass permit under the name of *nervosität*" (p. 353).

The explanation of the preceding passage is to be found in a section of Michelstaedter's thesis devoted to "the reduction of the person," in which he describes how man, in becoming "a social person," "has founded his life on the contingency of things and persons," whereby "all the progress of civilization is a regression of the individual" (pp. 109–110),[41] especially in that "any substitution of machines for manual labor stunts man's hands proportionately," and artisans and craftsmen "have been replaced by masses of sad and stupid workers in their factories, who know but one gesture, who are almost the last lever of their machines" (p. 112). A consequence of such a situation will be "illnesses of the limbs and in general muscular sicknesses because of inertia and atrophy, and those of the internal organs as well because they function in a void, without the balance that the vitality of the limbs gave to their activity. Connected with these, the diseases of circulation. . . . The sign that life is thus out of its regular course are the diseases of the nervous system—diseases of which society seems almost to boast" (p. 113). Michelstaedter's description of bourgeois, industrial society can be linked with Freud's *Civilization and Its Discontents*. It is indeed an indictment, a protest: in an imaginary "Speech to the People"[42] Michelstaedter envisages a future world "where *man* will reign—the working man, the man *healthy* in body and mind, the man who won't need unjust and complicated laws"; he ends with the exclamation "Farewell, brothers—long live work and justice—death to the *bourgeoisie!*" (p. 671). Michelstaedter advocates a strong, "total" individual and wants "the self and the world to be one" (p. 46), thus indicating that he nevertheless believes in a favorable prognosis and in a possible, though difficult, therapy.[43]

Svevo, in open disagreement with Michelstaedter and Freud,

[41] Cf. Eugenio Garin, "Omaggio a Carlo Michelstaedter," in *Studi goriziani* 24 (July–December 1958): 23–31, especially p. 26, where the connection is made with Hegel's phenomenology; see also Carlo Salinari, *Miti e coscienza del decadentismo italiano*, p. 274, for a comparison of Michelstaedter and Pirandello.

[42] The speech can be better understood if placed in the cultural climate that gave origin to literary protests, such as Ada Negri's poems on the "operaio superuomo."

[43] The most comprehensive critical contribution to date is Marco Cerruti, *Carlo Michelstaedter*; also see M. A. Raschini, *Carlo Michelstaedter*; Antonio Verri, *Michelstaedter e il suo tempo*; Cattaneo, *Esperienze intellettuali del primo Novecento*, pp. 13–29; and Giacomo Debenedetti, *Saggi critici, prima serie*, pp. 55–69.

does not believe in therapy. His skepticism is quite evident in "Soggiorno londinese," where he tells of a neurotic friend of his who was psychoanalyzed for two years and "returned from the treatment no less than destroyed: abulic as before, but with his abulia made more serious by the conviction that he, being made like that, could not act otherwise." The conclusion is to be expected: "As a treatment I didn't care for it. I was healthy, or at least I loved my sickness (if it is there) so much as to keep it as self-defense."[44] Further evidence is seen in his letters to Valerio Jahier, where, for instance, he says: "A great man that Freud is—but more for novelists than for patients."[45]

At the fictional level, Zeno is even more explicit: "I have finished with psychoanalysis," he says at the beginning of the last chapter: "After practicing it assiduously for six whole months I find I am worse than before . . . and I think that writing may help to work off the mischief that the treatment has done me" (p. 366). Later he calls psychoanalysis "a stupid illusion, a foolish trick that might take in an hysterical old woman" and "a quackery," while he refers to the psychoanalyst's attitude as "the intolerable conceit that allows him to group all the phenomena in the world round his new theory" (pp. 367 and 378).

It is time for the critic to begin gathering together the hints given by Svevo and to explore not so much psychoanalysis as literature, not so much disease as the act of writing.

Let us start with the title of the novel, *La coscienza di Zeno*, where the *signifiant* "*coscienza*" has different *signifiés*, different levels of meaning. The first can be traced to Freud's *Totem and Taboo*:

Taboo conscience is probably the oldest form in which we meet the phenomenon of conscience.

For what is "conscience"? According to linguistic testimony it belongs to what we know most surely; in some languages its meaning is hardly to be distinguished from consciousness.

Conscience is the inner perception of objections to definite wish im-

---

[44] Svevo, *Racconti*, p. 688.

[45] The letters to Valerio Jahier, 1927–1928, are in *Epistolario*, pp. 856–875 passim.

pulses that exist in us; but the emphasis is put upon the fact that this rejection does not have to depend on anything else, that it is sure of itself. This becomes even plainer in the case of the guilty conscience, when we become aware of the inner condemnation of such acts which realised some of our definite wish impulses.[46]

All the more strictly psychoanalytical behavior of Zeno, such as that seen in his relationships with his father, with Malfenti and Guido Speier, as well as with Ada and Augusta, and Carla and Carmen, should be considered on this level; included also should be his acts *manqués*, his distractions, and his psychosomatic diseases. Here Zeno's conscience is moral precisely in the sense indicated by Freud: it perceives a condemnation and projects it outward onto the others who become would-be and omnipresent judges—the objective correlatives of his sense of guilt.

On the other hand, one should also include on this level (at least partially) the irony with which Svevo describes all this behavior and these attitudes of Zeno, for through irony the oscillation of the conscience between the moral and the cognitive becomes apparent. In irony, the character is objectified through the *regards* of the others, is treated as if he were an "other"; the relationship between the narrator and the persona, in Jean Starobinski's words, is one of "exteriority," not of "solidarity or identity."[47] Thus Zeno's word is indeed at one and the same time remedy and poison—a word that cures his disease while establishing or positing it.

One consequence of the ambivalence of the word is Svevo's style, which seems a common, matter-of-fact, almost pidgin Italian, needing no ornaments or rhetorically elaborate structures to be extremely effective (the *signifiant* "disease," for instance, refers to physiological, psychosomatic, moral, metaphoric, and ontological *signifiés*); "but," as Montale pointed out, "it would be a mistake to believe that Svevo gains something when translated. The translations lost what I would call the sclerosis of his characters: Svevo appears elegant where he was fatiguing and profound, clogged and

---

[46] Sigmund Freud, *Totem and Taboo*, trans. A. A. Brill, pp. 89–90.

[47] Jean Starobinski, "Il pranzo di Torino," *Strumenti critici* 13 (October 1970): 243–287, now in *La relation critique*, pp. 98–153.

very free, a writer of all times but a Triestine of his difficult years."[48]
The linguistic "sclerosis" of Svevo's characters: the difficult process
of introspection, of revealing an inner knowledge through the
written word, could not be summed up in more precise, illuminating
terms.

A second level of meaning is the one defined by Derrida when he
refers to "conscience" as *présence à soi, perception de soi de la
présence*: "The privilege accorded to conscience, then, is the privilege accorded to the present; and even if the transcendental temporality of conscience is described in depth (as in Husserl), nevertheless the power of synthesis and of incessant gathering of traces is
accorded to the 'living present.' This privilege is the ether of metaphysics, it is the element of our thought in so far as it is caught into
the language of metaphysics."[49] It is almost obvious that this level
includes the temporal structure of *La coscienza di Zeno*, in which
time, "this fatality of the modern novel,"[50] is accorded a privileged
position. It is a strange time that can only be "reoccupied partially"
by the narrator and that "stagnates."[51]

Within time, the present tense is in its turn privileged to a certain
extent above the other tenses—past and future—that make up the
"mixed time" of man, "whose grammar instead has the pure tenses
which seem made for the beasts who, when they are not frightened,
live happily in a crystalline present."[52] This privilege, therefore, is
not blindly accorded by Svevo; on April 4, 1928, the very, very old
Zeno writes: "It is the future I am living now! And it glides away
without preparing the way for any other. So it is not even a true
present tense. It is outside time. Grammar does not possess a *final*
tense."[53] For Svevo, a demystifying author if there ever was one,

---

[48] Montale, "Italo Svevo nel centenario della nascita," p. 128.

[49] Jacques Derrida, "La 'différance,'" *Bulletin de la Société française de philosophie* 63 (1968): 73–120, quoted material on p. 89; now in *Théorie d'ensemble*.

[50] Montale, "Italo Svevo nel centenario della nascita," p. 128.

[51] Ibid., pp. 166–167.

[52] Svevo, *Further Confessions of Zeno*, p. 17.

[53] Ibid., p. 28. And p. 141: "It is no good looking for the present in calendars
or clocks; one consults them merely to establish one's relationship with the past
or to move with some semblance of consciousness into the future. It is I and the
things and people round me that constitute the true present." These passages

the present is certainly not "the ether of metaphysics." The present is privileged only because grammar lacks a final tense. At the beginning of the novel, Zeno states: "See my childhood? Now that I am separated from it by over fifty years, my presbyopic eyes might perhaps reach to it if the light were not obscured by so many obstacles. The years like impassable mountains rise between me and it, my past years and a few brief hours in my life" (p. 3). The years and the hours of the past are put on the same level; Zeno's eyes are presbyopic. It will be interesting to note that according to Georg Groddeck, one of Freud's precursors and disciples, "the inventor of the term Es [Id] and practically of the whole psychosomatic medicine,"[54] "the behavior of the Id is particularly strange when it is faced with old age and approaching death. It makes the eye presbyopic, it symbolically pushes away everything, even death, and prolongs life."[55] In any case, Zeno's temporal presbyopia indicates what really matters: the *now*, which is Zeno's present, and the tense irony as well. To quote Starobinski again: "Irony interprets the differential relationship of tenses in favor of the present; the ironist does not want to belong to his past. On the contrary, nostalgia interprets the differential relationship of tenses in favor of the past: the nostalgic does not bear to remain prisoner of his present." Therefore, in an ironic narration "the qualitative privileged tense is not the past but the present—the present of the narrative act in which knowledge, experience, fame authorize the writer to evoke his ignorance, his awkwardness, his shyness, with smiling condescendence."[56] These words can be applied to Zeno literally (only fame has little to do with his story, as opposed to Rousseau's), and they are important also because they point out the major difference between Svevo and Proust. For both authors, time is the object of *recherche*, but Marcel cannot bear to remain prisoner of his present, while Zeno does not want to belong to his past.[57]

should also be viewed in the context of Svevo's comedy, *La rigenerazione* (1928), which develops the same meditations on time, youth, old age, and death.

[54] Roberto Bazlen, *Lettere editoriali*, p. 81.

[55] Georg Groddeck, *Psychoanalytische Schriften zur Psychosomatik*, p. 13.

[56] Starobinski, "Il pranzo di Torino," pp. 243 and 256.

[57] Svevo was the first one to see the impossibility of this comparison with

To make Zeno's situation almost emblematic, Svevo relates the following scene:

I have stretched myself out after lunch in an easy chair, pencil and paper in hand. All the lines have disappeared from my forehead as I sit here with mind completely relaxed. I seem to be able to see my thoughts as something quite apart from myself. I can watch them rising, falling, their only form of activity. I seize my pencil in order to remind them that it is the duty of thought to manifest itself. At once the wrinkles collect on my brow as I think of the letters that make up every word. The present surges up and dominates me, the past is blotted out. (p. 3)

The imperious present is the tense of a diary or confession that unfolds almost imperceptibly throughout the novel, marking different present points above the Bergsonian *durée*; from them Zeno sees himself and takes stock in increasingly comprehensive spheres of understanding. For instance, one of the first images that strikes Zeno is that of the panting train engine, a seemingly inexplicable image but one that is then explained from the point of view of a later present moment that provides a perspective on the past:

While I sit writing, or rather engraving these tragic memories on my paper, I realize that the image that obsessed me at the first attempt to look into my past—the image of an engine drawing a string of coaches up a hill—came to me for the first time while I lay on the sofa listening to my father's breathing. That is just what engines do when drawing an enormous weight: they emit regular puffs, which then become faster and finally stop altogether; and that pause seems dangerous too, because as you listen you cannot help fearing that the engine and the train must go tumbling over heels down into the valley. How curious that is! My first real effort to remember had carried me back to the night that was the most important in my life. (p. 41)

It was, of course, the most important night in Zeno's life because it was the night when his father died, and it is related to the present

---

Proust: "It is impossible that a rude man like me resembles the most perfect product of such a refined civilization" as the French one (letter to Valerio Jahier of December 2, 1927, in *Epistolario*, p. 857). Cf. Debenedetti, *Il romanzo del Novecento*, pp. 537–558, on the relationship between Svevo and Proust and pp. 558–594 on the relationship between Svevo and Joyce.

of the narrator not at the end of a continuous temporal line, but
rather through an image that pops up while he sits "writing, or
rather engraving." This image is tremendously important not only
because it constitutes Zeno's self, in that it is a "parricide" word (in
Derrida's terms) emblematically posed at the outset of the novel,
but also because it indicates the temporal structure of the narration,
in that it corresponds to an isolated, privileged present that is
fleeting, always changing, and that will be replaced by another
present, equally isolated and privileged but different. Each chapter
uncovers (or rather occupies) the past in a different place (smoking,
the death of Zeno's father, the marriage, the wife and the lover, the
business partnership); each chapter is therefore not only centered
around a specific segment (spatial segment) of Zeno's life, but also
written from the point of view of a present tense that is always
moving forward, being postponed in time. Thus the Zeno who is
writing the last chapter (on psychoanalysis, indeed) is the same
Zeno who started off the first, but he has become very different:

> I ought to be cured, for they have found out what was the matter
> with me. The diagnosis is exactly the same as the one that Sophocles
> drew up long ago for poor Oedipus: I was in love with my mother and
> wanted to murder my father.
>
> I did not even get angry. I listened enraptured. It was a disease that
> exalted me to a place among the great ones of the earth; a disease so
> dignified that it could trace back its pedigree even to the mythological
> age! And I don't feel angry, even now that I sit here alone, pen in
> hand. . . . The surest proof that I never had the disease is that I have not
> been cured of it. (p. 367)

It is indeed Zeno, with pen in hand, who believes that he has the
"power of synthesis and of incessant collection of traces" of his past
life, while living his present: "It is only now that I feel myself
definitely detached from my preoccupation with health and disease"
(p. 386). It is Zeno who, after the outbreak of world war, reaches
the conclusion that he is not sick at all, that being well is "a matter
of conviction" and of "self-persuasion":

> I may have to put on a poultice now and then for some local ailment,
> but otherwise I force my limbs to keep in healthy motion and never

allow them to sink into inertia. Pain and love—the whole of life, in short—cannot be looked on as a disease just because they make us suffer.

I admit that my fate had to change, and my body to be warmed up by fighting and above all by victory, before I arrived at the conviction that I was well. It was my business that cured me, and I should like Dr. S. to know it. (p. 396)

What business is to Zeno on the fictional level, literature is to Svevo in reality. The author is concerned with the literary process, not with the psychoanalytical one: the latter, at most, could be (and in fact was) a pretext for the former:

[Dr. S.] has only studied medicine, and so has no idea what writing in Italian means to us who talk dialect but cannot express ourselves in writing. A written confession is always mendacious. We lie with every word we speak in the Tuscan tongue! If only he knew how we tend to talk about things for which we have the words all ready, and how we avoid subjects that would oblige us to look up words in the dictionary! . . .

And by dint of pursuing these memory-pictures, I at last really overtook them. I know now that I invented them. But invention is a creative act, not merely a lie. My inventions were like the fantasies of fever, which walk about the room so that one can survey them from all sides and even touch them. They had the solidity, the color, and the movement of living things. My desire created these images. . . . The doctor noted everything down. He said: "We have had this, we have had that," though we had really had nothing but graphic signs, mere skeletons of images. (pp. 368–369)

The words that are made up of letters in space and time, the graphic signs, the written words (although written in "Tuscan") opposed to the spoken ones (though spoken in dialect)—all point to the difference, and *différance*, between literature and life.

Svevo is aware of this difference/*différance*, yet the reader is not quite sure where the preference of the author lies. Life, certainly, is unforeseeable and most original, but without literature it is not really complete; literature is the expression of life and also its completion, its "supplement." On the one hand, Svevo could write in

1902: "By now I have definitely eliminated that ridiculous and harmful thing called literature from my life"; on the other hand, he could write in 1899: "In sum, outside the pen, there is no salvation."[58] And in 1928 he could make his "old, old man" Zeno state:

> Writing, . . . which I look forward to doing every evening just before taking my physic, will serve a hygienic purpose. And it is my hope that these pages of mine may contain the things I don't normally say aloud, because only in that way can the treatment be successful.
>
> Once before, I wrote with the same idea in mind—of being sincere, that is; and hygiene figured in it then, too, because my writing was intended to prepare me for psycho-analysis. The treatment failed, but the pages remain. . . . Time is crystallised in them and can always be located if one knows how to open at the right page. Like a railway timetable.[59]

Writing, as opposed to saying ("it is my hope that these pages of mine may contain the things I don't normally say aloud"), is clearly indicated as something different from life, in fact as something that is supposed to cure life, as a treatment. Writing becomes a *pharmakon*: it serves a hygienic purpose, but at the same time it is also a poison or a malady in itself. "The descriptions of lives—of which a considerable part is omitted: the things everyone experiences but no one ever mentions—become more intense than the lives themselves":[60] more intense, therefore unnatural, abnormal, like a fever perhaps. The intellectual disease of man, to be torn between the blind power of life and the clear force of reason, between lively chaos and deadly order, between action and contemplation, is stated again by Svevo in all its great and mysterious complexity.

But there is yet another level of meaning in the title *La coscienza di Zeno*. Svevo knew bourgeois society and Western culture well, and he was very critical (in his quiet, polite, yet powerful way) of them and their basic conceptions. One of these conceptions was, in Derrida's terms, the idea of the book considered as an "expression de

58 Svevo, *Racconti*, pp. 818 and 816.
59 Svevo, *Further Confessions of Zeno*, p. 16.
60 Ibid., pp. 16–17.

la vérité anthropothéologique (en un mot la conscience de soi de Dieu dans le s'entendre-parler absolu: la con-science)."[61]

Con-science: this is the third level of meaning in the title of Svevo's novel. Derrida points to the possibilities that Western civilization has left unexplored, opens up insights that seem to deny centuries of history, culture, and language, and advocates a broader vision of the literary and human universe: *le livre ouvert*. And so does Svevo, through a work of fiction, not a philosophic system.[62]

Ironical, skeptical, and compassionate, he portrays Zeno's attempts at *con-science*, and his failures. The greatest part of Zeno's life is inextricably intertwined with "death, desire and repetition," as Anthony Wilden puts it,[63] and Zeno is always postponing, exorcizing his own death by describing that of his father and those of his father figures, Malfenti and Speier. Similarly, Zeno is constantly looking for Ada, the model of love, health, beauty, and perfection, the woman who is always beyond his reach; and his love for her is recognized and confessed only at the very end of the novel when it does not exist any longer. It is part of the strategy of the narration, as well as of the unconscious, that Ada is often mentioned indirectly, but always in the most important moments of Zeno's life. For instance, when Zeno begins the psychoanalytic treatment he thinks of Ada's child rather than himself; in the chapter on the wife and the mistress Ada is more present than the other two women; the business partnership between Zeno and Guido is started and continued solely because of Zeno's attachment to Ada, so that it could be called, more appropriately perhaps, a love bond.[64]

---

[61] Jacques Derrida, "Le livre ouvert," p. 18.

[62] Bruno Porcelli seems to have Umberto Eco in mind when he speaks of *La coscienza di Zeno* as "an open work, able to render the always unforeseeable rhythm of reality in its externally disorderly aspect" ("L'evoluzione dell'ideologia e della narrativa sveviane," *Problemi* 17–18 [1969]: 767–782).

[63] Anthony Wilden, "Death, Desire and Repetition in Svevo's *Zeno*," *MLN* 84, no. 1 (January 1969): 98–119.

[64] The final confession is also given *en passant*: according to Dr. S., "Ada was quite right in regarding" Zeno's absence from Guido's funeral "as a final manifestation of dislike . . . He quite forgot that I was at that very moment engaged in *my labor of love* to save Ada's fortune" (Svevo, *Confessions of Zeno*, p. 377, italics added).

Actually Zeno's search is not just a simple search for a single woman; it is his very life:

And as I looked back over my life and my malady, I felt that I loved and understood them both. How much better my life had been than that of the so-called normal healthy man, who, except at certain moments, beats or would like to beat his mistress every day. But I had always been accompanied by love. Even when I was not thinking of my mistress, I still thought of her in the sense that I craved her forgiveness for thinking of other women as well. Other men leave this mistress disillusioned and despairing of life. I have never known life without desire, and illusions sprang up afresh for me after every shipwreck of my hopes, for I was always dreaming of limbs, of gestures, of a voice more perfect still. (p. 382)

But Zeno's failures at *con-science* are also described (in a way closely reminiscent of Michelstaedter's) in his recurring attempts to control time and space, language, and knowledge, by means of the alphabet, the dictionary, the calendar, and the university.

The alphabet includes all the letters that make up words, from *A*, as in Ada, to *Z*, as in Zeno—the alpha and the omega, the beginning and end of a very subjective world (and one is tempted to remember that at the outset of Svevo's work there is another *A*: "L'assassinio di Via Belpoggio"). Between *A* and *Z*, within the space of the alphabet, Zeno is looking for some sort of logical order that is obviously impossible to find and that, when it seems to exist, turns out to be irremediably removed from the irrational disorder of life: for instance, there is no logical relationship between his marriage proposals in alphabetical order to the Malfenti sisters and their names all beginning with *A*, a "far country" from his own; similarly there is no logical relationship between his desire to marry Ada and his actual marriage to Augusta. Only a few letters, then, remain as vestiges in Zeno's "book of memory": *C*, as in the name of his mistress, Carla; and *U.S.*, not as in United States but as in an "*ultima sigaretta*" marking the death of his father.

The dictionary contains and organizes in harmonious—that is, alphabetical—succession all possible words, except perhaps those that count most. "Who would have provided me with the true dictionary?" says Zeno, trying to justify a lie to Dr. S. (p. 377). He even writes in a dictionary, the very epitome of *literature*, the most memorable dates and facts of his *life*, such as "2 February, 1886. Today I finish my law studies and take up chemistry. Last cigarette!!"; or "During those hours of torment I wrote the date of the day in my dictionary against the letter C (Carla) with the comment: 'Last Betrayal.' But my first actual infidelity . . . only took place on the following day" (pp. 9 and 196).[65] As Freccero points out, the trouble is that the dictionary, although it should represent "the sum total of all of reality bound up in a single volume, with a sequential order (and therefore an apparent continuity) and an apparent rationale," actually "is dead because it is a spatial, discontinuous order, lacking the temporal flow of life just as the intellect is dead for analyzing atoms and for not being able to account for change."[66] The episode of the phlegmatic British cat unexpectedly attacking Zeno when he enters a bookseller's to buy (precisely) a dictionary is the fictional, funny, but eloquent sign of the dichotomy between the intellect and life.

Like the dictionary and grammar, the calendar tries to organize time but succeeds only in fixing "a true disorder in time" into a purely surface order: "except for July and August, December and January, there are no two successive months that have an equal number of days" (p. 381); only in a written note does time become crystallized, and then it "can always be located if one knows how to open at the right page. Like a railway timetable" (p. 16).

The university provides Zeno with a whole range of studies, from law to chemistry, studies that should constitute an encyclopedic knowledge. But he is emblematically unable to complete any of them, and he ends up a successful businessman who, among other things, with a last ironical twist, buys and sells incense, this other "ether of metaphysics."

[65] The same attitude is in "Lo specifico del Dottor Menghi," Svevo, *Racconti*, p. 534: "I find among my papers the bulletin on which I registered my discovery. It is dated *May fifth*. I am not superstitious, but the coincidence of dates is strange: May fifth is a date that recalls Napoleon, the man whose pulse was in unison with the watch."

[66] Freccero, "Zeno's Last Cigarette," p. 47.

The alphabet, the dictionary, the calendar, and the university, then, are elements of Western man's search for absolute knowledge, for an impossible totality that at the end is defined only by its own absence.[67] Derrida indicates that the whole of Western culture, based on phonetic, written words (*écriture*) that are not the original spoken Word and on an encyclopedic knowledge that is but a parody of the true absolute knowledge, should be aware of its limitations and ready to look for different ways of development; if the metaphor of the world as book is still valid, the book should be open, *le livre ouvert*.

Svevo concludes his novel *La coscienza di Zeno*, the book of twentieth-century man, "the newest Ulysses,"[68] precisely by leaving it open, by giving us the famous, terrifying vision of an apocalypse that today has become part of the concrete possibilities of mankind. By doing so, he was certainly more avant-garde (both in technique and ideology) than F. T. Marinetti, whose Futurist manifestoes and *parolibrismo* did not succeed in going beyond the phonetic structure of writing.[69] Svevo's apocalypse "concludes" a very precise narrative structure and an equally precise criticism of Western society, history, and culture. (The end of Antonioni's *Zabriskie Point* could be interpreted similarly.)

Let us examine Svevo's conclusion, which is the epitome of what Kermode calls "the sense of an ending." After foreshadowing what Rachel Carson has called the "silent spring" ("Our life today is poisoned to the root" and not only in a strictly ecological sense), he goes on to say:

But it is not only that, not only that. Every effort to procure health is in vain. Health can only belong to the beasts, whose sole idea of prog-

---

[67] Eduardo Saccone, "Furbank su Svevo," *MLN* 83, no. 1 (January 1968): 126–136. See especially p. 135.

[68] As early as 1926, in "Presentazione di Italo Svevo," Montale had written that the novel was the contribution of Italian literature to that group of books dealing with "the smiling and desperate atheism of the newest Ulysses: the European man" (*Lettere, con gli scritti di Montale su Svevo*, p. 111).

[69] An evaluation of Marinetti in relation to Derrida is in Fausto Curi, "La 'distruzione del modello lineare' e la letteratura d'avanguardia," *Lingua e stile* 5, no. 3 (December 1970): 447–456, now in his *Metodo Storia Strutture*, pp. 181–

ress lies in their bodies. . . . But spectacled man invents implements outside his body, and if there was any health or nobility in the inventor
there is none in the user. . . . The earliest implements only added to the
length of his arm, and could not be employed except by the exercise of
his own strength. But a machine bears no relation to the body. The
machine creates disease because it denies what has been the law of creation throughout the ages. The law of the strongest disappeared, and we
have abandoned natural selection. We need something more than psychoanalysis to help us. Under the law of the greatest number of machines, disease will prosper and the diseased will grow even more numerous. (pp. 397–398)[70]

Thus far Svevo's diagnosis is substantially similar to Michelstaedter's. It is developed from the early essay explaining the origin of
man's disease, "L'uomo e la teoria darwiniana," as Saccone has
shown,[71] and it can be compared today with some of Marshall
McLuhan's theories. But Svevo's words are much more impressive
than any scientific theory; they become a prophecy linking Zeno's
present with his future, which is our present potential destiny:

Perhaps some incredible disaster produced by machines will lead us
back to health. When all the poison gases are exhausted, a man, made
like all other men of flesh and blood, will in the quiet of his room invent
an explosive of such potency that all the explosives in existence will
seem like harmless toys beside it. And another man, made in his image
and in the image of all the rest, but a little weaker than them, will steal
that explosive and crawl to the center of the earth with it, and place it
just where he calculates it would have the maximum effect. [Are these

---

191; see also Brunella Eruli, "Marinetti, quale avanguardia?" *Il Ponte* 25, no.
10 (October 1969): 1303–1316.

[70] Cf. also pp. 394–395: "The open wound, as they soon began to call the Italian
front, in Austria, had broken out again and needed more matter to feed it. [The
original Italian is stronger than the translation: "La piaga *cancrenosa* . . . abbi-
sognava di materiale per nutrire la sua *purulenza*."] And the poor men advanced
toward it shouting and singing."

[71] Saccone, "Svevo, Zeno e la psicanalisi," pp. 72–74. Now see his *Commento a
"Zeno,"* a long and at times prolix study that is impossible to analyze here; Saccone shows that *La coscienza di Zeno* is the product of a "new rationality" based
no longer on the principles of identity and dialectics, but on those of repetition
and difference (p. 69).

not the so-called Doomsday machines, about which spectacled strate-
gists rave?][72] There will be a tremendous explosion, but no one will
hear it and the earth will return to its nebulous state and go wandering
through the sky, free at last from parasites and disease. (p. 398)

For Svevo, therefore, the disease of the individual, his failure in
intersubjective relations because of the weakness of his nature and
the abstractness of his thought, becomes the disease of society and
of history, the anguishing recognition that human reason cannot
explain life, cannot control a world deprived of a teleology (as J.
Hillis Miller points out in *The Disappearance of God*), and cannot
discover or cure the sorrow that lies behind our existence. Here
disease, more than a metaphor, appears indeed as an ontological
category.

By ending *La coscienza di Zeno* with a cosmic explosion, Svevo
not only points to the nothingness that does not conclude every
search (in the ancient Egyptian legend analyzed by Plato and
Derrida, Thot, the god of writing, was also the master of numbers,
the calendar, funeral rites, and death), but also leaves open the possibility for another, better mankind. The written word, which is
itself a "disease" of man, attempts a "cure" in the form of a paradox
for the other men, still parasites, to meditate upon.

Zeno's Apocalypse: a *pharmakon*.

[72] On the "Doomsday machines" it might be useful to consult the frightening
anthology edited by Donald G. Brennan, *Arms Control, Disarmament and National Security*.

4. Moscarda's Mirror

> *The* necessity of madness . . . *is connected with the* possibility of history.
>
> Michel Foucault, *Madness and Civilization*

> *It is conscience that gives a color of blood, a cruel note, to whatever act of the will, because it is clear that life is always someone's death.*
>
> Antonin Artaud, "Première lettre sur la cruauté"

The change of expression in my image was instantaneous, by reason of the spontaneity of my wrath; and this change was followed, with equal suddenness, by a bewildered apathy; as a result of all of which, I succeeded in beholding, there before me in the mirror, my body detached from my imperious soul. . . .

Who was that one? No one. A poor body, without a name, waiting for someone to take it.

But all of a sudden, as my thoughts ran like this, something happened to change my stupor to a looming terror. I beheld in front of my eyes, through no will of my own, the apathetically astonished face of that poor mortified body piteously decomposing, the nose curling up, the eyes turning over inward, the lips contracting upward, and the brows drawing together as if for weeping—they remained like that, in suspense for an instant, and then without warning came crumbling down, to the explosive accompaniment of a couple of sneezes. The thing had happened of itself, at a draught of air from some place or other, without that poor mortified body's having said a word to me, and quite beyond any will of my own.

"To your health!" I cried.

And I beheld in the mirror my first madman's smile.[1]

Vitangelo Moscarda, the last novelistic character created by Luigi

[1] Luigi Pirandello, *One, None and a Hundred-thousand*, trans. S. Putnam, pp. 36 and 39–40. Subsequent references will be to this edition.

Pirandello, is the protagonist-narrator of *Uno, nessuno e centomila*, a book that the author considered a true manifesto of his theatrical work.[2] Moscarda is alone in front of a mirror, searching for the stranger within himself, one revealed by his wife Dida's remark that his nose, instead of being straight, bends to the right.[3]

This remark, like many others, even insignificant ones, caused Moscarda to fall "into deeps of reflection" that rent his soul "from top to bottom and tore it inside out like a molehill, without any of all this being visible on the outside" (p. 15); the molehill, with its suggestion of an allusion to the unconscious, can be considered a rather explicit image of those "personality troubles" that Gaspare Giudice points out in Pirandello's characters: a sense of evanescence of the self, dissociation, ambivalence of knowledge, a perception of the defectiveness of one's personality, a sense of irreality.[4]

Moscarda's situation in front of the mirror is different from the typical and normal one: different, for instance, from that of Anna Rosa, who contemplates her body, attitudes, and expressions at the mirror "as a game, a momentary game of coquetry and flirtatiousness" (p. 245), far away from "anormality," but also from the seriousness, depth, and complexity that characterize the protagonist. While Anna Rosa embodies life without conscience, Moscarda is completely taken within the "sphere of conscience," which is, on the one hand, juxtaposed to life (as in Svevo) and, on the other hand, to nothingness (as in Michelstaedter). In Pirandello's system,

---

[2] Conceived of since 1910, *Uno, nessuno e centomila* was published in 1925 and was considered by Pirandello as "the novel of the breaking down of the individual personality," as well as "the bearer of the positive side" of his thought (Claudio Vicentini, *L'estetica di Pirandello*, pp. 238–240).

[3] Pirandello's essay on "L'umorismo" also deals with an ugly nose in relation to the mask, the dichotomy between being and nothingness, the problem of "seeing oneself living" (*Saggi, poesie, scritti vari*, pp. 152–155 and [on Cleopatra's nose] p. 159). Giovanni Macchia relates Moscarda's nose (as well as the fragmentary structure of the novel) to Laurence Sterne's *Tristram Shandy* (*La caduta della luna*, pp. 265–266).

[4] Gaspare Giudice, *Pirandello*, p. 403; also, pp. 403–404: "Neurosis has entered into Pirandello's theater sneakingly and branching off in a domain of imaginative possibilities," whereby his work "meets with his times, which are the most hysterically neurotic that ever existed."

this "sphere of conscience" is termed *lanternosophy*, an idea that he developed in 1908 in the essay "L'umorismo."[5]

The first logical conclusion that Moscarda draws from his wife's remark is that he does not know his own body well, so others must know him differently from the way he thinks he is; therefore, he must try to see himself as an other than self, redouble and verify himself. Hence the ritual of the mirror, which, however, from the very beginning leads toward "madness," as is shown by the image of the madman's smile concluding the quotation.

We must begin by ascertaining the semantic and metaphoric meanings of "image," "mirror," "madness," because, in his thoroughly modern version of the ancient myth of Narcissus bending over a fountain and annulling himself, Pirandello undoubtedly insists on the disintegrating aspect of the discovery of the self, and he has done so by portraying madness as a social concept or category. One could consider the following figure of a madman an emblem of the whole novel; he, as the objective correlative of the narrator, "must have just got out of bed with the insane idea of experiencing the voluptuousness of flight": "Exposed there to the fury of the wind, he was holding up, so that it might flap about his thin body, so thin that it sent a shudder down one's spine, his red woolen bed coverlet, suspended from and supported by his arms which were crossed under his shoulders. And all the while, he was laughing—laughing with a glint of tears in his bedeviled eyes, while his long reddish locks of hair flew about him, to this side and that, like licking tongues of flame" (p. 240). This madman in *Uno, nessuno e centomila* is an almost literal repetition of an analogous emblematic figure in *I vecchi e i giovani*, the novel that poses the historical foundations of Pirandello's disillusionment and consequent critical polemics.[6]

[5] On *lanternosophy* cf. Pirandello's remarks in *Saggi*, pp. 152–157, and *The Late Mattia Pascal*, trans. William Weaver, pp. 161–174; on the relationship between Pirandello and Michelstaedter, see Marco Cerruti, *Carlo Michelstaedter*, p. 143.

[6] Cf. Luigi Pirandello, *The Old and the Young*, trans. C. K. Scott Moncrieff, II, 286: "Several of them had been looking out, through one of those windows, at the

The *dédoublement de soi* implicit in the idea of Moscarda's image at the mirror points immediately and powerfully to the other idea always present in Pirandello's work (not in the theater only)—that is, the idea of the mask, which in turn points to the conception of reality as a social construction. But let us stay for a while at the level of the character: Moscarda seems to be the perfect literary specimen of a phenomenon described by Heinrich von Kleist in his puppet's theater; that is, he illustrates the "disturbances conscience provokes in man's natural gracefulness." This phenomenon is taken up again by Ludwig Binswanger (precisely in relation to Kleist's image of a young man at the mirror), and, through an anthropo-analytic explanation that is worth quoting, it is related to the idea of the mask:

In this *self-mirroring* one should see the *essential peculiarity* of mannerism, as a particular and characterized manner of stunning oneself. The key to understanding mannerism and contortion as privileged ways of an inauthentic being-in-the-world is therefore in the desperate *mirroring* of a "self," in the explicit *imitation* of a fashionable *model* (i.e., of a model belonging to the publicity of the self), of a *certain* social "type" or of an *artistic* manner. This imitation is both in the order of behavior and attire, expression, writing, speaking, and in the way of living and of making art. Yet the same thing is true for the contrary of imitation, that is opposition, since imitation and opposition imply the *dependence* on the publicity of the self.

What in Being as instrument is the mirror and mirroring, in the Being-in is the publicity of the self and the mirroring in it, in the sense of *conceptual* "reflection." . . . If the peculiar schema of reflection is "if-then," here reflection happens in this way: if *that* is a usual way of being for the publicity of the self, I adopt it, I make it mine, I imitate it, I accentuate it or transform it into its contrary. But, insofar as Being-

---

terrace of an old house opposite, upon which a poor lunatic seemed to be testing some secret joy, that of flight perhaps, exposed to the fury of the wind which sent fluttering round his body the yellow woolen blanket that had been draped over his shoulders: he was laughing with the whole of his wretched face, while his keen, demoniac eyes glistened with a film of tears, and the long locks of his reddish hair floated out on either side of him like flames."

in assumes this model or its opposite, insofar as it *reflects* on them, this model becomes something superimposed, a *mask*, a *shield*, a *veil*.[7]

Binswanger's remarks seem particularly fitting for Moscarda's initial inauthentic being-in-the-world, from the mirror to reflection, from rebellion to the mask.

Now, one must remember that the *signifiant* "mask" is present even in the first lines of the very first novel by Pirandello, *L'esclusa* (1893), where the "moth-eaten" face of Antonio Pentàgora appears "almost a mask";[8] there the *signifié* is naturalistic, expressive, while in *Il fu Mattia Pascal* it is metaphorical: "Let's be fair: I had got myself up like that for others, not for myself. Now did I have to go on living with myself in that masquerade?"[9] The meaning of this metaphor is explained by Pirandello in the "Warning" he added to the novel in 1921:

> But what if the *universally human* significance and value of some of my fables and my characters set in the contrast . . . between reality and illusion, between the individual's countenance and society's view of it, consisted . . . in this: that a socially abnormal situation is accepted, even when seen in a mirror, which in this case holds our own illusion up to us; and then we play it out, suffering all its pain, as long as the performance is possible behind the stifling mask that we have put on ourselves or that others, or cruel necessity, have forced on us; in other words, as long as beneath this mask some keenly felt feeling of ours isn't hurt there? Then the rebellion finally breaks out, and that mask is torn off and trampled underfoot. . . .
>
> The mischief then, if it exists, is there by desire; the mechanism, if there is one, is also there by desire, but not by *my* desire. The fable itself, the characters themselves demand it. . . . It is the mask for a performance, a game of roles; what we would like to be or what we should be, what we appear to others. What we really are, even we ourselves don't know beyond a certain point. The clumsy, inadequate metaphor of ourselves; the product, often badly put together, that we make ourselves, or that the others make of us. Yes, there is a mechanism in which

---

[7] Ludwig Binswanger, *Drei Formen Missglückten Daseins*. Quotations will refer to the Italian translation, *Tre forme di esistenza mancata*, pp. 223–224.

[8] Luigi Pirandello, *Tutti i romanzi*, p. 11.

[9] Pirandello, *The Late Mattia Pascal*, p. 102.

a person is, purposely, the marionette of himself, as I said before; and then at the end, comes the kick that knocks the whole theatre apart.[10]

This "warning" is fundamental for *Uno, nessuno e centomila*, too, precisely because, in postulating a character who in front of a (still-metaphoric) mirror discovers his mask and rebels against it, knocking "the whole theatre" of social structures apart, it points to Moscarda's initial as well as final situation.

From Claudio Vicentini's clear analysis we know that Pirandello, in forming his idea of the social construction, was influenced by the works of Alfred Binet, Giovanni Marchesini, Gabriel Séailles, Nordau, and Gaetano Negri.[11] But, we need to follow Debenedetti's lead and return to a consideration of Jung and his definition of the division of contemporary man between different and contrasting attitudes that depend on the milieu in which he works or lives: "He puts on a *mask*, which he knows corresponds to his conscious intentions, while it also meets with the requirements and opinions of his environment, so that first one motive then the other is in the ascendant. This mask, viz. the ad hoc adopted attitude, I have called the *persona*, which was the designation given to the mask worn by the actors of antiquity. A man who is identified with this mask I would call 'personal' (as opposed to 'individual')."[12]

It is to be noted that Pirandello speaks of a contrast between "an individual face and its social image," and that his whole work tends to uncover "the naked individual face under that mask," which is indeed "the clumsy, inadequate metaphor of ourselves."

In the long-distance dialogue between the scientist and the playwright-novelist, a critic intervenes authoritatively. Debenedetti, noting that Jung, "having to study the perturbations to which modern man is inclined, . . . resorts to a metaphor suggested by the idea of the face," states: "Metaphors are not born distractedly, above all they don't let themselves be used scot-free. The face is the

[10] Ibid., pp. 248–249.

[11] Vicentini, *L'estetica di Pirandello*, pp. 28–34 and 42–44.

[12] Carl Gustav Jung, *Psychological Types*, trans. H. Godwin Baynes, p. 590; this definition is quoted by Giacomo Debenedetti, *Il romanzo del Novecento*, p. 481.

visual metaphor indicating the attitude taken on by man in order to balance himself off with his *milieu,* both private and public. But then, we may infer, if the Other from within, if what Jung calls the internal object begins to disturb the Self adjusted to the external object, then the mask will be altered, and it will express the presence and the insidious annoyance of those disturbances."[13] Let us think of Pirandello and of the quotation with which this chapter began: Moscarda's two sneezes, and even more his madman's smile in front of the mirror, take on a tragic and premonitory value in their seeming comicality. They cohere perfectly with the "theory of the opposites" of Pirandello's *umorismo* and are in perfect emblematic consonance with Debenedetti's "character-man."

If, from the unconscious and individual aspects of the mask, we go on to consider the conscious and personal ones (that is, the collective or social ones), we shall first note that Pirandello has perceived a fundamental datum of contemporary sociology: the social construction of reality, the mask as a cluster of functions, as role. For instance, according to Berger and Luckmann:

The origins of any institutional order lie in the typification of one's own and others' performances, [which must] have an objective sense, which in turn requires a linguistic objectification. . . . In the course of action there is an identification of the self with the objective sense of the action. . . . That is, it becomes possible to conceive of the self as having been only partially involved in the action. . . . It is not difficult to see that, as these objectifications accumulate . . . , an entire sector of self-consciousness is structured in terms of these objectifications. In other words, a segment of the self is objectified in terms of the socially available typifications. This segment is the truly "social self," which is subjectively experienced as distinct from and even confronting the self in its totality.[14]

Berger and Luckmann go on to say that "the origins of roles lie in the same fundamental process of habitualization and objectivation as the origins of institutions"; since "*all* institutionalized conduct

[13] Debenedetti, *Il romanzo del Novecento,* p. 482.

[14] Peter L. Berger and Thomas Luckmann, *The Social Construction of Reality: A Treatise in the Sociology of Knowledge,* pp. 67–68.

involves roles," the latter "share in the controlling character of institutionalization," and therefore they "have a special relationship to the legitimating apparatus of the society," in that they help maintain "integration in the consciousness and conduct of the members of the society."[15] Another point should be emphasized in the sociological theory: the legitimating function of the persons who are important in the life of the individual is necessary for the conservation of the subjective reality of a member of society; these persons are an indispensable element in the member's "structures of plausibility": "The relative importance of the significant others and of the 'chorus' can be seen most easily if one looks at instances of *dis*confirmation of subjective reality. A reality-disconfirming act by the wife, taken by itself, has far greater potency than a similar act by a casual acquaintance."[16]

If one accepts the premise that the narrative impulse of the character originates precisely from an act of disconfirmation of Moscarda's reality by his wife, Dida, then the relevance of the sociological theory to the interpretation of Pirandello's art cannot be denied. The scene in front of the mirror is the initial fundamental episode. In this context, one also thinks of the contrast between the nickname Gengè, dear to the wife, and the name Vitangelo, so irremediably necessary, at least at the beginning, for the very identity of the character.

If we want to give credit to sociologists for their use of the concept of "the play of roles," whereby roles "*represent* the institutional order" in themselves and in their interrelationships, then it is equally undeniable that Pirandello's human and artistic intuitions have had a certain relevance for sociologists: "Only through such representation in performed roles can the institution manifest itself in actual experience. The institution, with its assemblage of 'programmed' actions, is like the unwritten libretto of a drama. The realization of the drama depends upon the reiterated performance of its prescribed roles by living actors. The actors embody the roles and actualize the drama by representing it on the given stage.

[15] Ibid., pp. 70–71.
[16] Ibid., p. 139.

Neither drama nor intuition exist empirically apart from this recurrent realization."[17] The great importance of this quotation can be understood in the light of Lucio Lugnani's remarkable analysis of *Sei personaggi in cerca d'autore*. Lugnani sees the contrast between characters and actors as symbolizing the contrast between the individual and society; the character-individual tries to affirm his history and autonomy in front of the actor-society. The actor, who once was wearing the mask, must follow the role, the part, the programmed and therefore coercive action.[18]

It is not necessary here to survey the places, the frequency, and functionality of the part in Pirandello's work. Suffice it to say that the part is the active, dynamic, and immediately recognizable manifestation of the mask, and that as such it is the focus of the crisis of the individual who rejects both mask and part for the sake of his own individuality, of his truest and most intimate identity. To quote from *Uno, nessuno e centomila*: "I knew, moreover, that by placing myself under new conditions of life, by appearing to others tomorrow as a doctor, let us say, or a lawyer, or a professor, I should no more than before have found myself either one to all or an individual to myself, as I went about in the garb and performing the functions of any one of those professions. Everything was now comprised in the horror of being locked within the prison of any form whatsoever" (p. 215).

But the crisis of the individual, the polemic against bourgeois society, its institutions and roles (a ferocious polemic that Jean Genet must have taken into account in his *Le balcon*), has an inexorable development in Pirandello. Starting with the acknowledgment that society is a construction, he arrives at a belief in its destruction through an element that is an integral and necessary part of this construction: mental disease with its whole therapeutic and repressive apparatus. Here, too, one thinks of the symbolic value of the actors when, in the final scene of part 1 of *Sei personaggi in cerca d'autore*, they remain "closed to any feeling of compassion for or participation with" the characters, and in fact they

[17] Ibid.
[18] Lucio Lugnani, *Pirandello: Letteratura e teatro*, p. 125.

show themselves determined to "refuse that intrusion as enormous and monstrous, and to consider it as madness. The only extenuating circumstance conceded by society to its rebellious victims is in fact mental disease: it is a cruel benefice, because it does not absolve, it does not forgive, and does not welcome back, but it rejects those furious, crying or arguing rebels into a life term of solitude, it isolates them forever into a closed space, like lepers or madmen." Referring to Auerbach, Lugnani concludes that the characters "illuminate the *figural*, not realistic sense of *madness*" in Pirandello's polemic.[19]

Let us go back first to the beginning of Pirandello's polemic against society; it is nature, the countryside:

Let us say, then, that what we call peace is to be found within ourselves. Doesn't it seem so to you? And do you know where it comes from? From the very simple fact that we have just now left the town, that is, a world that is *built*—houses, streets, churches, squares—not for this reason alone, however, because it is *built*, but also because we no longer live for the sake of living, like these plants, without knowing how to live, but rather for something that is not and which we put there, for something that gives meaning and value to life, a meaning, a value which here, at least in part, we succeed in losing, or of which we recognize the grievous vanity. (pp. 67–68)

The city world is horrible: "all is invented and mechanical, assembling and construction, a world within a world, a manufactured, agglomerate, adjusted world, a world of twisted artifice, of adaptation, and of vanity, a world that has a meaning and a value solely by reason of the fact that man is its artificer" (pp. 71–72). On the contrary, as Voltaire well knew, "it would be well, if there

---

[19] Ibid., pp. 132 and 128. Cf. also p. 44: Lugnani recalls Russo's remark that D'Annunzio preferred the term *demenza* (which "has something ecstatic, shadowy, hallucinatory, sweet, visionary") rather than *pazzia* (which "has something too bodily and violent, liable to break the thin veils that entice his aesthetic curiosity") and concludes that Pirandello's use of the latter is an example of his "art of things" (rather than "of words"); in cultural terms, "madness as alienation is almost a modern and significant topos, in its diversified forms—alibi and fancy, *paradis artificiel* and a pact with the devil or psychological labyrinth."

were a little more understanding between man and Nature. Too often, Nature takes a pleasure in knocking down all our ingenious constructions. Cyclones, earthquakes—But man does not give up. He rebuilds, rebuilds, stubborn little animal that he is. Everything to him is material for building. . . . Man takes even himself as material, and builds himself, my dear sirs, like a house" (p. 75).

When Moscarda at the mirror sees his image as a "stranger," he reaches his mask, the construction of himself made by the others in the city world; but with his first madman's smile he begins to destroy this social construction. "Necessary madness," Moscarda says, giving us an important indication of the value to be attributed to his disease. Pirandello uses the *signifiant* "madness" as it is taken in common, social usage and changes its *signifié* completely—figuratively, metaphorically, and semantically. In the novel *Uno, nessuno e centomila*, more than any other of his works,[20] the mirror is the instrument for this operation.

In the scene already examined, the mirror functions figuratively as the concrete object that causes Moscarda to recognize his madman's smile (but in this recognition, doubt is already implicit); metaphorically, it is the comparison necessary to turn the term "madness" into the term "conscience" (a conscience lucid like a mirror of madness; madness as a mirror of conscience): "By arousing in me, little by little, as if it had been a sort of game, the will to exhibit myself as different from one of the hundred-thousand in whom I lived, it at the same time altered in a hundred-thousand ways all my other realities. It was inevitable, if you think it over well, that this game of mine should yield the fruit of madness. Or, better, this horror: the consciousness of madness, as clear and fresh, good people, as fresh and clear as an April morning, as shining and precise as a mirror" (p. 130).

Semantically, the mirror confirms Moscarda's new situation, as well as Pirandello's fierce criticism: "But it was precisely because

[20] According to Giudice, *Pirandello*, p. 191, the mirror in Pirandello is one of "the metaphors of depersonalization" (another is the telescope): "In *I vecchi e i giovani* all the principal characters, one after another, and one unknown to the others, are led sooner or later in front of a mirror in order to be reduced to larvae."

I possessed this accurate-mirroring consciousness that I was mad. You, on the other hand, who go down this same street without caring to take any notice of it, you are the wise ones, and your wisdom grows as you raise your voices to shout at the one who walks beside you: 'I this one? I like that? You are blind! You are mad!' " (p. 142). The conclusion is that madness, as it is considered in contemporary bourgeois society, not only is erroneously treated in order to preserve social stability (one thinks of Ervin Goffman's and Franco Basaglia's works, or of the book with the frightening title *La fabbrica della follia*, "the factory of madness"),[21] but also, precisely for this reason, should be completely revaluated; in fact it should be (paradoxically but not too paradoxically) taken as a model of behavior and judgment. This is the meaning of the scene in which Moscarda kneels down in front of Firbo and Quantorzo, his banker friends who with "fear in their eyes" believe him to be mad; and he, repeatedly knocking his head on the floor ("bump, bump"), addresses them as follows: "You, not I—understand?—to your wife—understand?—ought to be doing this! And I, and he, and all the others, to all the so-called madmen—ought to be doing this! . . . Then go—go there where you keep those people locked up; go, go and listen to them talk! You keep them locked up because it's more convenient for you!" (p. 150). This scene is a resumption, on a less solemn note, of an analogous one in *Enrico IV* (1922) in which the "great Masked One," the protagonist "oscillating between a clinical report and a metaphysical message, so clearly hysterical besides being Hamletic and tragic,"[22] obliges his four fake Counsellors to kneel: "I order you to go down on your knees before me! And touch the ground three times with your foreheads! Down, down! That's the way we've got to be before madmen!"[23] In the play, a true "monument to madness,"[24] this scene is cleverly prepared for by a long

---

[21] On this point see Chapter 1, note 25.

[22] Giudice, *Pirandello*, p. 402. Also see Maurizio Del Ministro, "Interpretazione di 'Enrico IV,' " *La Rassegna della letteratura italiana* 75, no. 1 (1969): 16–26; on p. 23 he speaks of "a physical wound become spiritual laceration."

[23] Luigi Pirandello, "Henry IV," in *Naked Masks: Five Plays*, trans. Eric Bentley, p. 190.

[24] Giudice, *Pirandello*, p. 354.

monologue in which Henry IV deals with the semantic-social value of words: "That's the way public opinion is formed! And it's a bad look out for a man who finds himself labelled one day with one of these words which everyone repeats; for example 'madman,' or 'imbecile.' "[25] Then, the revelation that Henry IV is not at all mad leads to the perfect semantic equivalence of madness and sanity, while it allows Pirandello to criticize from the very roots the social system in which, on the one hand, the sane/sick dichotomy is often used to control and repress and, on the other hand, madness is only seen as a menace from the unconscious for the individual as well as a threat against society by the irrational:

You feel that this dismay of yours can become terror too—something to dash away the ground from under your feet and deprive you of the air you breathe! Do you know what it means to find yourselves face to face with a madman—with one who shakes the foundations of all you have built up in yourselves, your logic, the logic of all your constructions? . . . One must see what seems true to these hundred thousand others who are not supposed to be mad! What a magnificent spectacle they afford, when they reason! What flowers of logic they scatter![26]

It seems clear that what most interests Pirandello here is not madness considered as a mental disease and as such explored and studied, but rather madness as the fascinating, inscrutable, nocturnal side of man, an element that is potentially present in each of us and always ready to destroy the constructions on which the idea of human society is built.[27] It is precisely for this reason that contemporary sociology, while recognizing the precariousness of subjective identity, states that "the integration of the realities of marginal situations within the paramount reality of everyday life is of great importance, because these situations constitute the most acute threat to taken-for-granted, routinized existence in society."[28]

[25] Pirandello, "Henry IV," p. 190.

[26] Ibid., pp. 192–193.

[27] Of course, in this attitude of Pirandello's the well-known biographical datum of the jealous hysteria and madness of his wife Antonietta is a determining factor: see Giudice, *Pirandello*, especially pp. 247, 255, 297, 302, and 353.

[28] Berger and Luckmann, *The Social Construction of Reality*, pp. 90–91. The sentence continues: "If one conceives of the latter as the 'daylight side' of human

A premonitory echo of this idea can be found in the dramatic situation created by Pirandello, one in which the whole problem is led back to the human root of everyone's existential solitude: "I would never wish you to think, as I have done, on this horrible thing which really drives one mad: that if you were beside another and looking into his eyes—as I one day looked into somebody's eyes—you might as well be a beggar before a door never to be opened to you; for he who does enter there will never be you, but someone unknown to you with his own different and impenetrable world."[29] Notice that here madness ultimately functions as a pretext in a discourse that concerns the human condition; that the *par excellence* social act—that of looking, of the contact between two pairs of eyes—becomes a vehicle of incommunicability, a mirror of alienation; and that through it the deep and painful metaphor of the "beggar before a door never to be opened" is originated—a metaphor that is the medieval, historical situation of Henry IV and Matilde; but above all it is the figural one of "Henry IV" and the Marchioness, two characters called upon to realize, literally to live, that metaphor on the stage in Pirandello's play entitled *Enrico IV*.[30]

The tragedy of the character Henry IV is that, although he clearly sees how many men lose their individuality because of their

---

life, then the marginal situations constitute a 'night side' that keeps lurking ominously on the periphery of everyday consciousness. Just because the 'night side' has its own reality, often enough of a sinister kind, it is a constant threat to the taken-for-granted, matter-of-fact, 'sane' reality of life in society. The thought keeps suggesting itself (the 'insane' thought par excellence) that, perhaps, the bright reality of everyday life is but an illusion, to be swallowed up at any moment by the howling nightmares of the other, the night-side reality. Such thoughts of madness and terror are contained by ordering all conceivable realities within the same symbolic universe that encompasses the reality of everyday life—to wit, ordering them in such a way that the latter reality retains its paramount, definitive (if one wishes, its 'most real') quality."

[29] Pirandello, "Henry IV," p. 193.

[30] Also see Lugnani's remarks on *Sei personaggi in cerca d'autore, Pirandello*, p. 134: "The official theater (that is, official and social life) does not admit intruders improvising without a script, without knowing how to recite. . . . The *Character*, who has come out of a very precise history, out of an irreparable breach with men, vainly knocks at the door of those men, he vainly asks to be readmitted in his new appearance, distinct from them, different from them."

respective social roles ("... ah, that dress of theirs, this masquerade of theirs, of course, we must forgive it them, since they do not yet see it is identical with themselves"), he nevertheless finally remains fixed as a mask forever.[31]

But, as Binswanger noted, "to exist *as a mask*, that is, not behind but *in* a mask (a role) is the direct opposite of authentic existence and authentic community":[32] Henry IV's life is therefore a "form of failed existence"; it is mannerism. At the end of *Uno, nessuno e centomila*, Moscarda will be able to free himself from the mask that the world wants to impose on him, but he will pay an enormous price for a still-ambiguous result; in contrast, Henry IV deliberately enters forever the mask he had chosen. In both cases, Pirandello's critical stance is unmistakable, even at the stylistic level; it is conveyed through a sort of artistic mannerism that reflects the psychological mannerism of his characters-spokesmen.

Hans Hoffman's studies on mannerism "are based on 'experiences of our time,' because in our time individuality has lost its supreme validity and has witnessed the advent of the 'collective' in its place."[33] Thus it will be clear why I resort to a revival of style set as a working hypothesis.

First of all, let us recall the importance of role, status, ceremonial, mask, and grimace in the mannerism studied by Binswanger, and let us add the tendency of mannerist painting (noted by Hoffman) to abandon "the model of reality to let psychic links, symbolic relationships act with greater force":[34] some of these elements—from the mask to such symbolic relationships as the mirror or the door closed before the beggar—have already been analyzed as fundamental components of Pirandello's universe.

Another characteristic of mannerism is that it manifests itself above all in those historical periods when "the temporal content of an epoch" seems to become exhausted, when "the anguish for the fading away of any 'meaning' " seems to become predominant.[35] In

[31] Pirandello, "Henry IV," p. 205.
[32] Binswanger, *Tre forme di esistenza mancata*, p. 237.
[33] Ibid., p. 170.
[34] Ibid., p. 171.
[35] Ibid., pp. 173–174.

this context, too, one can speak of mannerism in connection with Pirandello, the author of *I vecchi e i giovani*, the witness of the waning of the nineteenth century and of the "drama of the *petite bourgeoisie* come out of the *Risorgimento*,"[36] the implacable critic of the society born in Italy with the twentieth century, the sharp consciousness of the crisis, the writer incapable of suggesting a positive alternative, an opening toward the future, if not in artistic (that is, stylistic) terms.

Remembering the theatrical revolution of *Sei personaggi in cerca d'autore*—which Wylie Sypher called "The Cubist Drama,"[37] that is, an undeniably expressionist type of theater—one might question the correctness of my recourse to mannerism in explaining Pirandello's style. This recourse does not seem unwarranted, especially when one recalls that Walter Benjamin, in his essay on Kafka, quoted the mannerist painter El Greco, "patron saint of the Expressionists," and his gesture of "tearing open" the paper sky in "the World Theatre."[38] It is the same gesture as that in Pirandello's *Il fu Mattia Pascal* and, if it were realized, Orestes would be transformed into Hamlet, thus marking the difference between classic and modern tragedy.[39]

[36] Corrado Alvaro, "Presentazione," *Novelle per un anno* by Luigi Pirandello, I, 19; and on the same page: "Pirandello wrote the second part of the work to which Verga was aspiring." It will be remembered that according to Montale it was Svevo who continued Verga.

[37] Wylie Sypher, *Rococo to Cubism*, pp. 289–294, now also in *Pirandello*, ed. Glauco Cambon, pp. 67–71.

[38] Walter Benjamin, *Illuminations*, p. 121.

[39] Pirandello, *The Late Mattia Pascal*, p. 139: "If at the climax of the play, just when the marionette who is playing Orestes is about to avenge his father's death and kill his mother and Aegisthus, suppose there were a little hole torn in the paper sky of the scenery. What would happen? . . . Orestes would still feel his desire for vengeance, he would still want passionately to achieve it, but his eyes, at that point, would go straight to that hole, from which every kind of bad influence would then crowd the stage, and Orestes would feel suddenly helpless. In other words, Orestes would become Hamlet. There's the whole difference between ancient tragedy and modern, Signor Meis—believe me—a hole torn in a paper sky." Note that Diego Fabbri made a reference precisely to this "hole in a paper sky" in considering Pirandello "like Orestes: his classicism corroded by dialectical thought." See "Pirandello ieri oggi domani," a round table with Diego Fabbri, Alberto Moravia, Guido Piovene, Edoardo Sanguineti, Luigi Squarzina,

But let us continue to examine *Uno, nessuno e centomila*. In what sense and within what limits it is possible to speak of mannerism in Pirandello's style will become clear if one considers, on the one hand, his "soliloquy" (a critical operation conducted by Marziano Guglielminetti with remarkable stylistic results)[40] and, on the other hand, his use of the grotesque. The latter aspect interests us more, because, behind the prevalent expressionistic achievement (an expressionism à la George Grosz, to be sure), there is a mannerist component, the grimace, the winking.

The grimace is connected with the mask and hence to the central, emblematic image of the mirror. Here is a significant example:

> I glanced at myself in the clothespress mirror with an irresistible self-confidence; I even winked my eye by way of signifying to that Moscarda there that we two understood each other, all the while, marvelously well. And it is but the truth I am telling you, when I say he winked back, by way of confirming that understanding.
>
> (You, I know, will inform me that this was due to the fact that the Moscarda in the mirror there was I; and by so doing, you will be proving to me yet one more time that you know nothing whatever about it. . . .) (pp. 206–207)

Notice that the character's winking at himself corresponds to his winking at the reader. In contrast, here is a true grimace, introduced by an address to the reader-accomplice but completely developed at the level of the characters (i.e., Moscarda and the notary): "Do you get it, now? I simply had to wink at him, too, by way of signifying roguishly, '*Look underneath! Look underneath!*' And what's more, Heaven help me, I had to stick out my

---

and Manlio Cancogni in *La fiera letteraria* 42, no. 30 (November 1967): 15–20; quoted material is on p. 20. This same "hole in a paper sky" could be taken as an emblem in order to differentiate Pirandello from contemporary theater, which he has prepared and forerun, to be sure, in that a "skeptical" knowledge makes him "feel helpless" in front of every violence, cruelty, or tragedy.

[40] Marziano Guglielminetti, *Struttura e sintassi del romanzo italiano del primo Novecento*, p. 114: "Pirandello's soliloquy is the first nonrhetorical, indeed suffered, narrative structure, giving voice to the condition of crisis in human relationships and of confusion in values, typical of this century's European literature."

tongue, when he least expected it, and suddenly screw up my nose, all without any maliciousness and as a kind of game, by way of altering at one stroke that image of me which he believed to be the true one" (pp. 134–135).

The following represents an example of purely stylistic winking (pertaining to a theatrical soliloquy) without the figurative and narrative equivalent of the grimace: "Was I not in all truth, setting out to play a dirty trick upon Signor Vitangelo Moscarda? Yes, good people, that is what it was! a dirty trick (you will have to excuse all these winks on my part, but I have need of winking, to wink like this, since, not being aware just what impression I am making upon you at this moment, I may be able thus to obtain a hint)" (p. 131). Winking, then, is related to the initial semantic field of the mirror: to look at, to see, to see oneself, to be seen by others, by the others' eyes; to turn one's eyes and face toward the others to recognize them and to make oneself recognized in the respective individualities. The text moves from the mask to the mirror, from the *poétique du regard* to the theatricality of soliloquy.

In particular, this *poétique du regard* is an indispensable element for the final term of Pirandello's stance we have examined so far, that is, madness; it can be found even in the following oxymoron, "dark light," which is so meaningful—within the semantic context including darkness and light, blindness and vision—for the juxtaposition between reason and nonreason, health and sickness, normality and social pathology:

I could feel at that instant how tangled those inner motives were, how subtle and contorted by my many long fits of meditation; and so far as that goes, they were no longer clear even to myself, agitated and wrathtorn as I was, in that dark light which glowed with so terrible a fixity, and which I had come upon thus solitarily; while there was nothing but darkness for all the others, who went on living blindly and securely in the habitual plenitude of their emotions. At the same time, I realized that, by revealing so much as a single one of mine, I should appear hopelessly mad to each of this pair—for example, the fact that, up to a short while back, *I never had seen myself* as they had always seen me, that is, as one who continued to go on living tranquilly if whimsically upon the

usurious proceeds of that bank, without having openly to acknowledge the fact. (pp. 195–196)

The image of the dark light immediately reminds one of an analogous statement from "Cogito et histoire de la folie," in which Derrida defends the unity of human thought ("the hyperbolic boldness of Descartes's Cogito: whether I am mad or not, *Cogito, sum*. In all the meanings of the expression, madness is therefore but a *case* of *thought—within* thought"), and this defense is concluded by precisely the same oxymoron that Pirandello uses: "We have tried not to blow out that *other* light, that black and so little natural light: the wake of the 'powers of senselessness' around the Cogito."[41]

The whole of Derrida's argument is actually based on a protest against the "originary violence" through which the word has freed itself by imprisoning madness, that is, by instituting a symmetrical opposition between reason and its opposite. Here is then the importance of Moscarda's mirror. In the context of the *poétique du regard*, it points to the image of the other-than-self, of the double; it provides a literally symmetrical mirroring of the two selves of man's character (spirit-body, sanity-madness) divided by the heredity of Western dualistic metaphysics. As Bontempelli noted years ago: "Pirandello's man is completely overwhelmed by the same metaphysics he had invented in order to be snatched from the swamp of senses and to reach understanding."[42]

It remains then to analyze the term that in Pirandello is juxtaposed in a polemically symmetrical way to madness, that is, "conscience" or, just to remain within the semantic field of the mirror, "reflection." This term is linked with an element of violence that is fundamental for an understanding of Pirandello's *vision du monde*, because it is in fact his rebellion against the society in which he lives and in which his characters act.

Giudice has stressed repression and explosiveness as essential elements of Pirandello's temperament, showing how in his human and artistic world violence and destruction (though complemented

[41] Jacques Derrida, *L'écriture et la différence*.
[42] Massimo Bontempelli, "Pirandello o del candore" (1937), in *Introduzioni e discorsi*, p. 24.

by the opposite movement of compassion) and above all "parricide" have a very marked place.[43] In this connection, it seems worth applying some of Derrida's statements on Artaud to Pirandello: "A murder, however, is always at the origin of cruelty, of that necessity called cruelty, and first and foremost a parricide. The origin of the theater, as it should be restored, is a *coup* against the illegal holder of the logos, against the father, against the god of a scene that is subjected to the power of the word and of the text."[44] Hence the word-gesture of the theater, the hieroglyphic writing "in which phonetic elements are coordinated with visual, pictorial, and plastic elements."[45] In Pirandello's novel the visual, pictorial elements are coordinated with the phonetic ones. This characteristic is probably derived from the repression and explosiveness noted by Giudice, who in fact suggests "a stylistic research à la Spitzer (with Freudian emphasis)" to confirm his insights.[46]

Although the Freudian aspect is not so important here, Giudice's suggestion is valuable for the definition of Pirandello's style in relation to violence—which is a verbal violence, fixed above all in the grimace of the character. In this connection, one should remember the description of Moscarda's sneezes in the initial episode; it seems a good example of those words that Giudice calls "strangely agglutinating" (*arrovesciare, all'indietro, contrarre, aggrottar, crollar* in the original Italian), "awkward and hooded with syllables and double consonants" (*a scatto, lo scoppio, una coppia*); the final result is that these words "always try an irregular, excessive, sometimes angry and sadistic, semantic effort."[47] In the grimace of the sneezing Moscarda, the visual, pictorial, and plastic elements are totally connected with the phonetic ones, originating a language that is already theatrical, of a theater of cruelty.

But violence is not exhausted at the purely semantic or stylistic level. Suffice it to remember that even in *Uno, nessuno e centomila*

---

[43] Giudice, *Pirandello*, pp. 87 and 345. Also Debenedetti speaks of "an exploding of single words" in Pirandello's style (*Il romanzo del Novecento*, p. 401).

[44] Derrida, *L'écriture et la différence*, pp. 307–308.

[45] Ibid., p. 301.

[46] Giudice, *Pirandello*, p. 87.

[47] Ibid., pp. 87–88.

the protagonist is significantly an orphan, his thoughts about his dead father are certainly not benevolent, and his whole behavior is meant to destroy what his father had built, in order to be able to affirm himself against him. For instance:

The thing, I fancy, quite likely happens to all sons. It is to be noted that there is something mortifying for us and all but obscene where our fathers are concerned. . . . Our birth, our detachment, our cutting off from him, is a common enough case, was possibly foreseen, and yet was an involuntary thing in the life of that stranger, the indication of a deed, fruit of an act, something in short that actually causes us shame, arousing in us scorn and almost hatred. And if it is not properly speaking hatred, there is a certain sharp content that we are now conscious of in our father's eyes also, which at this second happen to meet our own. We to him, as we stand upright on our feet here, with a pair of hostile eyes, are something that he did not expect from the satisfaction of a momentary need or pleasure, a seed that he unknowingly cast, a seed standing upright now on two feet, with a pair of popping snail's eyes that stealthily survey him and judge him and prevent him now from being wholly what he would like to be, free, *another man* even with respect to us. (pp. 96–97)

Moscarda's parricidal language should be noted here ("obscene," "shame," "scorn," "hatred," and those "popping snail's eyes" that carry the *poétique du regard* to a grotesque paroxysm). This language is similar to Zeno's, which is less explicit and less violent, but for which the notion of parricide through the word (in Derrida's terms) has an equally great importance.

If it is true that a large part of Pirandello's work can be understood as a reaction to his father, as an explosion of violence against any psychological repression caused by the family, society, and authority, then perhaps even from this point of view one can speak of a *théatre de la cruauté*, which will later have in Antonin Artaud its most eloquent and impassioned theoretician,[48] with a passion

---

[48] The notion of "total theater" is also relevant for Pirandello (Gino Rizzo, "Luigi Pirandello in Search of a Total Theatre," *Italian Quarterly* 12, no. 45 [Summer 1968]: 3–26).

impossible to feel for Pirandello-Hamlet, taken as he is in the circle of dialectical reason, rather than in the whirlpool of nonreason.

As for Moscarda, the acts through which he realizes his first rebellion (the eviction and the donation) are described in a chapter entitled "The Explosion" (p. 158); more particularly, one should see the scenes involving the kick to the little dog Bibì and Moscarda's subsequent "fierce and maniacal merriment" (p. 178) and the other scene when Moscarda, "the light of his eyes" having gone out again (p. 197), shakes his wife Dida and throws her on an armchair "like a fragile doll." Then he reflects with anguish: "The vivid shuddering horror inspired by my violence was evident in my hands, which were trembling still. I became aware, however, that this horror was due not so much to the violence I had exerted as it was to the blind upward surge within me of a feeling and will which had ended by *giving body* to me: a bestial body, which had struck terror and endowed my hands with violence. I was becoming 'one' " (p. 201). Aside from the play element in Moscarda's mannerist language the close relationship of self-awareness and violence stands out clearly in these words. Moscarda, who is first of all reacting against the frightful violence of usury (that is, of the capitalist system that has "disqualification for mental illness" among its weapons), must also reject conscience in that it too causes violence; it is, like society, a construction.

Pirandello's refusal of society brings him back to the first datum of the fundamental dichotomy: countryside, nature. It is a return to origins that is also a regression to an impossible childhood and purity. Moscarda concludes the parable of his madness by coherently refusing his identity, name, and possessions and by donating all his resources to the building of an asylum for beggars in the countryside; he is a bit like the protagonist of the play *Lazzaro*:[49] "If I gave all and opposed nothing, it was because I was by now as

---

[49] See Debenedetti, *Il romanzo del Novecento*, pp. 351–352: "In the attitudes of this donor [Diego in *Lazzaro*] there is also something of the revenges and self-conquering achieved in the same manner by the frustrated protagonist of *Uno, nessuno e centomila*: the most significant, in this sense, of Pirandello's novels."

far removed as could be from anything that might have a meaning or a value for others; I not only was absolutely alienated from myself and from everything, but I had a horror of remaining in any manner *someone*, in possession of something" (p. 265). Moscarda's alienation here is indeed existential; to use Debenedetti's words on Mattia Pascal, it is "his impossibility of coinciding with a self that he does not know" and that orders him only negatively, imposing on him "a state of availability that makes him prey of all the alienations,"[50] just as the greatest representative of the "gratuitous gesture," Gide's Lafcadio. Moscarda's alienation began in front of a mirror, was increased by the discovery that "to know one's self is to die" (p. 247), and is concluded by the rejection of self-awareness, by preventing thought from making "the void that goes with the vanity of building things" (p. 268). That is why Moscarda refuses his mask, everything that is personal, and renounces the action that gave origin to his whole story: "I have not since that day glanced in a mirror, and the desire to know what has become of my face and the whole appearance that once was mine does not so much as enter my head" (p. 266).

Together with the mask and the mirror, Moscarda rejects the most social aspect of man, his language: "No name. No memory today of yesterday's name; of today's name tomorrow. If the name is the thing, if a name in us is the concept of everything that is situated without us, if without a name there is no concept, and the thing remains blindly indistinct and undefined within us, very well, then, let men take that name which I once bore and engrave it as an epitaph on the brow of that pictured me that they beheld; let them leave it there in peace, and let them not speak of it again" (pp. 266–267). Moscarda's *epochè* is complete. One could say that he achieves what, according to Debenedetti, Mattia Pascal had failed in, that is, "remaining between parentheses, not re-entering a society that remains fundamentally, structurally equal to the one from which

---

[50] Ibid., pp. 318, 333, and 384. On the contrary, Geno Pampaloni speaks of the "gratuitous act" in Svevo as one "more complex and modern" than Gide's, as "the objective situation of man in unreality. . . . Zeno *receives* unmotivated responses from life" ("Italo Svevo," in *Il Novecento*, vol. 9 of *Storia della letteratura italiana*, ed. Emilio Cecchi and Natalino Sapegno, p. 523).

he had exiled himself, . . . and prolonging his exile *sine die*, perhaps forever, closing himself up in a Trappist convent or becoming a hermit."[51] Moscarda's solution has found imitators in contemporary literature, for instance in the narrator of Giuseppe Berto's *Il male oscuro*, who retreats to the country at the end of his long and tormented psychoanalytical confession. But its importance is that of having indicated rather than solved the terms of a problem that is not only Pirandello's, but also a general and contemporary one. As Carlo Salinari pointed out, on the one side there is

the feeling of the anarchic condition in which modern man lives, of the lack of an organic social tissue that would support him and link him to other men, of the rule of things on men that are outside his will, of his unavoidable *defeat*. . . . As a *consequence*, the other *motif* appears, i.e., *nature*, as the place and condition of living juxtaposed to *society*: as the latter is chaotic, the former is organic; as one is anguished in its awareness, the other is simple, unknowing, and happy. Which means that there are in him [Pirandello] the two terms of the crisis of contemporary conscience.[52]

Moscarda, like Svevo's Zeno or Musil's "man without qualities," is then a typical anti-hero of twentieth-century literature. Born of a parricidal word, dedicated to a punctilious and destructive self-analysis,[53] accustomed to "see[ing] himself living," having passed "from one course to another without drawing any profit from any of them" (p. 98), Moscarda has searched for a total knowledge that has been revealed as impossible to discover. In the confrontation between conscience and intersubjectivity, Moscarda has learned of the impenetrability of others and the breaking down of the self;

[51] Ibid., p. 339.

[52] Carlo Salinari, *Miti e coscienza del decadentismo italiano*, p. 280. It is also for this reason that, according to Antonio Gramsci, Pirandello "contributed much more than the Futurists . . . in bringing about a modern 'critical' attitude opposed to the traditional nineteenth-century 'melodramatic' one" (*Letteratura e vita nazionale*, p. 52). Then see Piero Raffa, "Criteri per la lettura del linguaggio teatrale di Pirandello," in *Avanguardia e realismo*; and for a negative stance, see also Gian Franco Venè, *Pirandello fascista*.

[53] The dichotomy between knowledge and action in Pirandello is dealt with by Giovanni Cecchetti, "Beneath Pirandello's *Naked Masks*," *Forum Italicum* 1, no. 4 (December 1967): 244–258, especially on p. 253.

he has understood how limited the human instrument of communication—language—is in confronting the ever-fleeting reality of life. Thus, for him it is better to give up the epitaph of his name and to live in a pantheism in which his individuality (not his persona) can finally assert itself by annulling itself into the Whole.

Pirandello rightly arrives at this extremely open result in a short chapter entitled "No Conclusion," where the *poétique du regard* is abandoned—the poetics of those eyes, agents of conscience, that are used not only to see others and reality, but also to read the *écriture*, the written words of literature: "And all, from second to second, is as it is, revived to take on appearance. I quickly turn my eyes in order not to see again anything coming to an apparitional halt and dying" (p. 268).

The *poétique du regard* (and hence the mirror, conscience, city, society, health, and literature) is replaced by what could be called a poetics of hearing (that is, bells, life, countryside, pantheism, madness, and the Word):

The city is far away. There comes to me occasionally, upon the vesper calm, the sound of its bells. I, however, no longer hear those bells within me, but without, ringing for themselves and perhaps trembling with joy in their resounding cavities, in a beautiful blue sky filled with a warm sun, to the twittering of swallows or swaying heavily to wind and cloud, so high, so high, in their aerial belfries. To think of death, to pray. It may be that there is one who yet has need of this, and it is to his need that the bells give voice. I no longer have any such need, for the reason that I am dying every instant, and being born anew and without memories: alive and whole, no longer in myself, but in everything outside. (p. 268)

The cosmic sound of bells does not conclude *Uno, nessuno e centomila* exactly as the foreseeing of a cosmic explosion does not conclude Svevo's *La coscienza di Zeno*. Moscarda too has arrived at "a God who was an enemy to all buildings" (p. 241), and as such, perhaps, similar to the ancient Ra-the-Speaking-God, diffident in front of Thot, the god of writing.

The annulment of the individual conscience into the universal one, into pantheism, is the logical conclusion of Pirandello's stance toward the crisis of faith in anthropocentric teleology, a crisis theorized in the essay "Arte e coscienza d'oggi" and explained in its historical, as well as absolute, components.[54]

I do not believe that too much emphasis should be placed on Pirandello's pantheism per se as an autonomous and positive position. Rather, it should be considered as an indication, a metaphor of something other than and different from contemporary society.[55] A confirmation can be found in the final phase of Pirandello's writing and above all in the unfinished play *I giganti della montagna*, where, according to Lugnani, the *scalognati* ("unlucky ones") foreshadow

a group that is beyond every tragedy, that has cut every social relationship and has even dismissed the habit of reason that veiled the tragic syllogistic solitude of the *character*. This group has accepted dreams, madness, magic inventions, poetry, in short the most typical terms of ancient abnormality, and has called them life, and considers them normal, and accepts their irrationality down to the bottom. Coward is the one who reasons! However, the price is very high; there is in fact an only price to be paid in order to surmount tragedy and the human: "One can have everything only when one has nothing."[56]

Moscarda, who has not even a mirror in which to look at himself, certainly is a predecessor of these *scalognati* anti-heroes and of their irrational utterances, which today are carried on in the old affluent society by many of the young. As for the future, it is per-

[54] On this point one should read the whole first part of Vicentini's book, *L'estetica di Pirandello*, particularly pp. 15–21 and 38–56.

[55] The same point can now be found in the stimulating analysis made by Renato Barilli and founded on an intelligent application of Leslie A. White's "culturology" (*La linea Svevo-Pirandello*, especially pp. 216–220 ["The Poetics of the Mirror"] and 220–226 ["A Lay-mundane Mysticism"]). A different interpretation, rooted in sociologic as well as anthropologic criticism, is offered by Roberto Alonge, *Pirandello tra realismo e mistificazione*, in which Pirandello is shown to oscillate between "conscience" and "myth"—the myth of the eternal return to Mother Earth.

[56] Lugnani, *Pirandello*, p. 198. For differing critical evaluations of *Uno, nessuno e centomila*, see, on the negative side, Arcangelo Leone De Castris, *Storia di Pirandello*, pp. 198–202, and, on the positive side, Antonio Di Pietro, *Luigi Pirandello*.

haps important to recall the last novel Pirandello wanted to write
but never did. In Bontempelli's words,

On this side of the world that Pirandello stripped naked . . . human
society cannot find but total destruction or a new beginning. . . . In that
novel, which should have been entitled *Adamo ed Eva*, because of a
sudden cosmic cataclysm the earth remains [almost] uninhabited; only
a boy and a girl are left, in a condition to be able to live on, and with
the destiny to start the repopulation of the world anew, and to begin
history again. Adam and Eve, then: but Adam and Eve with a civilization behind their backs, instead of in front of them. The whole of Pirandello's work was the premise for this work, it was the preparation for
a renovating cataclysm.[57]

Pirandello's unaccomplished cataclysm seems indeed to echo
Svevo's final apocalypse and to confirm its epistemological value.

[57] Massimo Bontempelli, *Introduzioni e discorsi*, pp. 14–15.

5. The Pen, the Mother

The disease of language should be one of those that see death near and emanate an odor of final judgment, otherwise life, the disease of Being, cannot be reflected in it.

Guido Ceronetti, "È ancora
possibile scrivere versi galanti?"

The greatest force inheres in that writing which, while engaged in the most audacious of transgressions, continues to uphold and to acknowledge the necessity of the interdict system (namely, science, philosophy, history, etc.). Writing is always traced between these two faces of the limit.

Jacques Derrida, *L'écriture
et la différence*

The master without words has grasped his sharp, shining pen.

A straight incision on the surface color of saffron, from the epigastrium down to the umbilical region. Small red drops point the course of the scalpel, without consequences—the adrenaline! A white stratum appears, the connective tissue that has been made anaemic just before and that further incisions now open until the wound is dilated to a double ogive, whose margins have some colors, from blood to waxen. The margins of the frightful lozenge distill their brief vermilion pain, which is immediately cleaned with a gauze by the assistant surgeon.

And here is the precise lucidity of the scissors, to penetrate and divide that pink serum-filled flat sheet, almost swollen by the fullness of the viscera it still hides and contains. It is the shining of an act that is usual for the operating surgeon, bent over the unbelieved nakedness, inner to the formal nakedness we know. . . .

The viscera were taken and extracted as a shapeless sequence of soft

enigmae (for me); their pink, red, whitish and yellowish colors told
me these viscera belonged to the primary and central activity of living
nature. They were a nongeometrical expression of the living "I," which
had been only plasma organized during the years by a differentiating
idea—or such it seemed in the image. The surgeon's hand lifts this "I"
above the gauzes and the tweezers, he "exteriorizes" it in the clarity of
the electric lights, and searches, searches it as if he wanted to find in it
some obstinate reticence, a stubborn, ancient simulation. . . . The intimate, nonreplaceable organic mechanism appears manifest to him and
his team in the swift clear-sightedness of their long-trained acts; on the
contrary, it appears perturbed, shapeless, a red and inane superfluous-
ness, the distress of a ripped-up unbaptized puppet, to my knowledge,
to me, ignorant of every anthropological matter, of any tangle, without
memory of past studies, scarce, uncertain. . . .

Into the infamous mess of "externalized" life, routed out of its cavern
as a prey in horror, the white man, now, insinuates his needles. He insinuates the point of his unperturbed knowledge into that heap of flaccid
tripes. . . . The man saws: slowly he saws, and ties. Small, immune
nurses, with immune tweezers, hand him one after another the daring,
attentive needlefuls necessary for that demonic patch. . . .

His dialectic is manifested in his silent acts; it is a biological remaking, a rethinking of nature's construction through the needles, a rewilling, a restoring Form. . . . For this restoration, the surgeon uses a practice unrealized by Being, not foreseen by nature. He operates with nature's complicity, above it.

By profaning the secret darkness and the interior of the person, the
healer has made its physical scheme manifest: he has read the idea of
nature in the heap of the slimy appearances. Over the stretched, dehu-
manized body, he insists with the tacit acts of his whiteness, which
appears to me almost as a high and mute mother or matrix of resurrection. I think of our ancient paintings, Saint Ann over the Daughter, and
Her over the livid body of the Son.[1]

These are the essential phases of a surgical operation performed by
Professor Carpiani in Milan in 1940 and described by Carlo Emilio
Gadda. It is an "anastomosis," which is, according to the etymology
of the technical term, "a direct connecting of the small intestine

[1] Carlo Emilio Gadda, "Anastomòsi," in *Le meraviglie d'Italia: Gli anni*,
pp. 260–261 and 264–268. Subsequent references will be to this edition.

back upward to the stomach, and this is an admirable language, which the Greeks, with their eternal words, have been able to concede to the manifesting necessity of sciences, even after centuries" (p. 263).

No doubt Gadda's text is emblematic for the theme of literary diseases. The levels at which we may read it range from the simple and elementary one of technical and medical positivism to the subtler and less obvious one of literary metaphors, where we pass through images and situations that are typically Gadda's and that find a remarkable enrichment and deepening precisely by their being placed in such a meaningful context.

I do not believe it is necessary to insist too much on the first level of reading. The text, even in the original title with which it first appeared in Milan's paper *L'Ambrosiano* ("Ablazione di duodeno per ulcera"), is a technical description made with the rigorous punctilious precision worthy of a handbook for anatomy students. Even the most absent-minded reader will not fail to notice the scientific, anatomical, and technical terms woven into the description.[2] These terms are important because, according to Gadda, they confirm the validity and the vitality of "the contributions of techniques" to literary language in a particular, in fact a specialized, field.[3] His vision is not at all a *regard médical*: there is in it something other and different that, going beyond the scientific status of the words through which it is manifested, posits the text in its literariness.

First of all, the atmosphere of the operation is removed, distanced from the very beginning; it takes place in an almost mythical elsewhere: "I would think I recognize, in a cell or in a strange hypogeum of ancient Egypt's centuries, the unperturbed performers of an embalmment, who on the corpse of King Amenhotep are performing the unusual and unspeakable, yet necessary, acts of a consecrating compassion" (p. 258). The recourse to the rite of embalm-

[2] As a significant contrast, one recalls the surgical operation on a foot in Flaubert's *Madame Bovary*.

[3] On this point, see Gadda's "Le belle lettere e i contributi espressivi delle tecniche" (1929) and "Lingua letteraria e lingua dell'uso" (1942) in *I viaggi la morte*, pp. 77–91 and 93–99, respectively, especially p. 97.

ment, with the sacred and mysterious quality connected with it, is not without reason if one remembers that, for the ancient Egyptians, Thot, the god in charge of funeral ceremonies, was also the god of medicine, numbers, and writing. Gadda "de-scribes" a surgical operation that is literally performed in the presence of death and in which the modern surgeon "seems to go through a ritual," to fulfill "the necessary acts" (p. 262), acts not dissimilar from the ancient ones.

Another element, one of a moral character, accompanies these acts, beginning with the preliminary washing of the surgeon's hands—completed with "the serene care of one who has reached the knowledge of the ends and the means," whereby "the gesture of the ancient Roman official loses the ancient meaning" and becomes the function of one "who will exclude the evil from the darkness of the body, and after exact minutes he will reassemble the reasons of life" (p. 259).

A third element, one of an aesthetic-historical character, is added to modify the apparent scientific status of the description: Gadda, the profane, in front of the "shapeless heap of bowels," of the "poor guts" of the patient, remembers "the trash of flabby things that become a scheme in the fantastic anatomical tables of Hundt's *Anthropologium*, in the gratuitous ribbon's knots of Peyligk's *Philosophiae Naturalis Compendium*, rather than the truthful, admirably clear drawings of the painter and anatomist Leonardo da Vinci, who was able to portray the tangle of the bowels's turns with beauty and evidencing lines" (p. 264). Actually Gadda identifies with Leonardo (the subtitle of a famous book of his is *Disegni milanesi*) and joins him "in a sort of gnosiological polemics, which he performs on swelling buboes with straight cuts, with the cold lucidity of a surgeon" (p. 223).[4]

[4] See Gadda's remarks in "Una mostra leonardesca," in *Le meraviglie d'Italia*, p. 222: "Leonardo above all is a marvelous designer: everyone knows that. He used to draw every form and appearance of the world that revealed itself so neatly to him," exactly as Gadda does, one is tempted to say. In fact, p. 227: "One could infer that a hand, not expert of drawing, would forget the abdominal curves in the abject tangle of the indistinct, but Leonardo cannot do away with a sailor's knot, and 'must' portray the curves *as* they are, therefore telling us,

Another element, however, distinguishes Gadda's text: affective participation. It is the author's eyes that, beyond "the margins of a frightful breaking" made by the surgeon, together with him but with a certainly nonscientific attitude, watch "the flabby and slimy secret of creation, . . . the sacred viscidity of that which is the prime *I* and in the second place thought" (pp. 262–263); it is a "consecrating compassion" that makes Gadda refer to the patient as a "poor Harlequin" (p. 266), a "late specimen of the human species" (p. 268), "a ripped-up, unbaptized puppet" (p. 265). Gadda's affective participation culminates in a beautiful lyrical image that would not be expected in the middle of the description of a surgical operation: "A dismay satiates me: tiredness has muddled my knowledge, has bandaged it with distant, lost desires, which float fatuously on contingency; I would like to walk on the beach, and drink the indigo of the sea again, and recognize the untouched bodies of the living who lose their memories in the sun" (p. 267).

At this point, however, it is necessary to underline what at once likens Gadda to the surgeon and at the very same moment distances him most greatly: the word. Gadda's word almost imperceptibly transforms the surgical operation into a cognitive one, and the latter into a literary operation. A general remark by Olga Ragusa can be applied with particular effectiveness to *Anastomòsi*: "in Gadda there is an added metaphysical dimension, the work serving not only to depict reality, however apparently deformed, but also to epitomize the process of knowledge."[5]

The ritual and sacral aura of the ancient embalmers and the modern physicians is the aura of the man of every time as he faces

---

after all, *what* they are. His graphic precision then acquires an enlightening value, a true 'thrust toward progress' . . . The work of Italian anatomists is already in full swing. And Leonardo, imitating them, cuts up corpses, and portrays them in a stupendous way. So the Gaddian Anonymous in the Magliabecchian Code xvii, sheet 17, remarks about him: 'et già ne dixe aver fatta notomia de più de xxx corpi tra maschi et femine de ogni età.' " The identification between Gadda and Leonardo becomes explicit in the "Gaddian" Anonymous.

[5] Olga Ragusa, "Gadda, Pasolini, and Experimentalism: Form or Ideology?" in *From Verismo to Experimentalism*, ed. Sergio Pacifici, pp. 239–269; quoted material is on p. 265.

the mystery of nature, the body, death—the irrational, in sum. Gadda's pen accompanies the surgeon's scalpel in his search, and that ancient, sacral aura surrounds both men: one thinks again of the "frightful lozenge," of the "unbelieved nakedness, inner to the formal nakedness we know"; but at this precise point a totally literary mechanism is turned on, the analogical word, the metaphor. The surgeon "insinuates the point of his unperturbed knowledge into that heap of flaccid tripes"; "his dialectic is manifested in his silent acts"; "he has read the idea of nature in the heap of the slimy appearances," while "his daring needlefuls" will "enter the thought of nature." Furthermore, the process of literalization makes the electric resector become "almost a new pencil of our times" (p. 262); and just at the beginning of the operation, in the culminating moment of the sacral ritual that must lead to the discovery of an equally sacral mystery, here "the master without words has grasped his sharp, shining pen." Here Gadda, master of the word, identifies completely with the surgeon Carpiani, master without words, and has put his sharp, shining pen into the surgeon's hand, or rather has put himself in the latter's place, in order to perform a difficult literary and cognitive operation. The surgeon is Gadda, the scalpel is the pen. Thot, the ancient god of embalmments, recalled from the very beginning, is again, here and now, the god of writing.

Exactly as the surgical operation is "a biological remaking, a rethinking of nature's construction through the needles, a rewilling, a restoring Form," by using "a practice *unrealized* by Being," so the writer's (any writer's) operation is added on to reality, realizes a practice of Being, is in itself a remaking, a rethinking, a rewilling, a restoring *form*. The word, indeed, is both supplement and *pharmakon*. Like the surgical operation, the word restores form to the "tangle" in the "heap of livid appearances" that are searched in the inside of anatomy.

With these remarks we have come to a further level of reading and of critical examination: the level directed to discovering and analyzing the elements that constitute Gadda's literary operation. As they appear in the long passage from *Anastomòsi* quoted at the beginning of the chapter, these elements are the following: (1) the organic "tangle," or life's "mess"; (2) juxtaposed to it, the "prime *I* and in the second place thought," or the "living I, which had been only plasma organized during the years by a differentiating idea"; (3) the "evil" closed in the "darkness of the body"; (4) the "unperturbed knowledge"; (5) the "whiteness" of the surgeon, juxtaposed to the "secret" and organic "darkness" and suggesting the idea of the mother or "matrix of resurrection," which calls to mind a painting of Saint Ann (done by Leonardo among others) and which points to an Oedipal complex that is fundamental in Gadda. He recognizes it as such, but apropos another author, of course.[6]

As any attentive reader would expect, these thematic and structural elements of *Anastomòsi* must be understood in order to comprehend Gadda's whole work; they peremptorily point from a text to *the* text, and they form a signifying chain that supports the entire narrative texture with implacable rigor.

The organic tangle or life's mess is the raw material, but also the primary origin, the prerequisite of Gadda's cognitive and literary operation, as well as of a very precise trend in modern art, as Morse Peckham and Francesco Arcangeli have shown in different contexts. According to Arcangeli:

The implicit meaning of the organic and modernly natural form of the Informal is, probably, that man, before being a political and social animal, is a man in the biological sense. Of course this biology, reaffirmed after the imposing contributions of humanism and the Christian conception, has a deeply dramatic meaning; it is an enthusiastic and at the same time desperate questioning of the secret of life. After all, is not art's questioning an intuitive reply to the daring inquiry of molecular biology into the secrets of life? By virtue of insight and historical position, art adequately replies to the breakthroughs of science. Art, by realizing itself, proposes itself as a value of life.[7]

---

[6] Cf. "Psicanalisi e letteratura," in *I viaggi la morte*, p. 60: "In Marcel Proust, however, the Oedipal relationship is extended to his grandmother, to his maternal grandmother. To him, the grandmother actually represents the eternal sense of motherhood: exactly as in our painting the succession—and I should say the descent—of the mothers and the lives, which, playing on three terms, begins with St. Ann and is extinguished in Christ."

[7] Francesco Arcangeli, *Dal Romanticismo all'informale*, pp. 33–34.

In *Anastomòsi* we see the best example of organic tangle in its most elementary, secret, biological manifestation: life pulsating inside the human body.

But the notion of tangle is for Gadda much more complex than that and could perhaps be compared with Borges's "labyrinth" in its gnosiological implications. Gian Carlo Roscioni, in his fundamental monograph, *La disarmonia prestabilita*, devotes an entire chapter to "The Cognitive Tangle" and examines the system tangle-mess (with its related conspicuous lexical derivates) in all its possible connections and implications, from *vision du monde* to style. According to Roscioni, Gadda's mess is not "a metaphysical datum or an intellectual scheme, an exercise-symbol of the mind desperately trying to discover a meaning, a result for the inquiry and the learning; rather it is the acknowledged, unavoidable impenetrability of reality in front of all the efforts toward an organic, thorough arrangement."[8] The notion of tangle (or mess) appears as a notion of totality underlying all the phenomena; in a literary context, it becomes "either a mimesis of the real deformation, or the deliberate breaking down of an apparent order, preparing the creation of a new reality."[9] The best accomplishment based on Gadda's notion of tangle is perhaps the novel bearing the emblematic title *Quer pasticciaccio brutto de via Merulana*.

In keeping with his premises, Gadda incorporates the notion of the "I" within the more general and deeper notion of tangle and realizes a constant reduction of the "differentiating idea" of the individual. In *Anastomòsi* not even the face of the patient is seen, nor is his name mentioned: he is "deprived of every superstructure of civilization," he is unfit "to represent his past rank or quality" (p. 257), he is reduced to "a purple knot" of "viscid and flabby things" in the surgeon's hands, and he is "under the scissors and the needles like the threadbare clothes of the poor in the hands of a

[8] Gian Carlo Roscioni, *La disarmonia prestabilita: Studio su Gadda*, p. 82.

[9] Ibid., p. 95. On the contrary, according to Renato Barilli, Gadda has not completely freed himself from the naturalistic reason (especially in his use of the pathological as a transgression of the norm), and he also has some decadent strains (*La barriera del naturalismo*, pp. 105–128). Cf. also Guido Baldi, *Carlo Emilio Gadda*.

patient tailor" (p. 268). The "I" appeals to Gadda's compassion only insofar as it is an organic knot. But in other writings the reduction of the "I" is much more explicit and total than in *Anastomòsi*. For instance, in "Come lavoro":

Recent physical theories (that is, physicomathematic, biophysic, psychological, psychiatric ones) have flooded against the idol "I," this pole: as a muddy and overflowing flood they have almost succeeded with divine permission in submerging the gullible head. . . . My best cognition has been suggesting that I drop this childish hypotyposis of the writer-pole, to give it up, to leave it to the trash of someone else's repertoire, with benign but undefeated disposition. Each of us appears to me to be a knot, or lump, or tangle of physical and metaphysical relationships (the distinction has only a value of expediency).[10]

Gadda isolates some of the relationships in this tangle in the light of recent scientific developments, thereby going beyond the biophysic level of the organic knot so primary in *Anastomòsi*:

The so-called normal man is a knot, or skein or tangle or snarl, of neuroses undeciphered by himself, so dovetailed (*enchevêtrées*), so fitted (*emboîtées*) into one another, that finally they coagulate into a pebble, an unbreakable brain: rock-brain or rock-idol: the document-proof, the best one can have, of the existence of normality. . . .

Actually, the difference between the normal and the abnormal person is only this one: that the normal does not have an awareness, not even a metaphysical suspicion, of his own neurotic or paraneurotic states, . . . while the abnormal sometimes reaches a discretely clear intelligence of acts, causes, origins, primary form, development, final sclerosis, and cessation of his neuroses together with his own death.[11]

Here are, clearly formulated, the foundations of what is perhaps

---

[10] Gadda, *I viaggi la morte*, pp. 10–11. The polemic is taken up again in the same book in "Emilio e Narciso," especially p. 262 ("the I, the most braggart-like among personal pronouns") and p. 265 ("the straight-neck pronoun, the first person pronoun, the happy one among women, the eminent among men: the one that says I about himself").

[11] Ibid., pp. 23–24. Also, on p. 47 ("Psicanalisi e letteratura") Gadda speaks of "the entangled complex of causes and occasional causes, both biological and mental, which Freud tried precisely to disentangle, to bring on the table under the pitiless light of analysis."

Gadda's masterpiece, *La cognizione del dolore,* a work in which
the author, setting anatomy aside, proceeds to the knowledge and
then the criticism of the whole social and psychoanalytic, ethical
and historical reality.

To understand *La cognizione del dolore* it is first necessary to go
back to "La casa," a piece written in 1932 in which Gadda speaks
of himself as "Duke of Good Cognizance" and "Prince of Analysis"[12] and in which he recalls Ludovico Ariosto's satire of the pear
tree (solid and lasting) and of the pumpkin (vain and short-lived)
in order to underline the fundamental quality and way of being of
the author; the irony of the aristocratic titles and of the moral-
literary quotation perhaps explains the remote genesis of the name
of the protagonist, Gadda's alter ego, Gonzalo Pirobutirro d'Eltino.
(Incidentally, this name could also be written Del Tino, with a
macaronic as well as psychoanalytical displacement.)[13]

But the first text that should be recalled to explain *La cognizione
del dolore* is "Novella seconda," originally "Matricidio" (1928). It
is a short story that was inspired by contemporary events and that
of course remained unfinished, like the later novel. The author becomes the ex officio defender of a young matricide who was often
called by the papers "chivalric hidalgo" because of his manners and
origins.[14] Hidalgo is precisely one of Gonzalo's titles and implies all
the related background of a fantastic and very real South America.
From the sketches of both the short story and the novel one knows
what the direction, the obsessive focus of Gadda's imagination, was
to be: "Tragic scene of the dying mother who feels that the son is
in the other room and calls him. She does not understand, she believes that the son is an accomplice. She dies."[15]

---

[12] Gadda's *La cognizione del dolore,* originally published in installments in
the review *Letteratura* between 1938 and 1941 (the same period as *Anastomòsi,*
which dates back to 1940), is translated by William Weaver as *Acquainted with
Grief.* Subsequent references will be to this edition. Gadda's "La casa" is in
Novella seconda; quotations are on pp. 138 and 152 respectively.

[13] See the scene of the symbolic parricide, when Gonzalo steps on his father's
portrait "as if he were pressing grapes in a vat" (p. 181).

[14] Gadda, *Novella seconda,* p. 160.

[15] Ibid., p. 171.

Let us briefly examine a few passages from *La cognizione del dolore*. First of all, Gonzalo is presented as the epitome of the seven capital sins, but actually he immediately appears as a character in desperate search of an absolute, incapable of compromises (like Michelstaedter who, were he alive, would be almost a contemporary of Gadda's):

> Germanic he was in certain manias for order and silence, and in his hatred for greasy paper, eggshells, and lingering at the door in formalities. In a certain inner torment in wanting to swim against the current of meanings and causes, in a certain disdain for superficial veneer, in a certain slowness and dullness of judgment, which seemed in him more like an inhalation before a sneeze, and in turbid and tardy synthesis, never with flashing ray of parrot-gold color. Germanic, above all, was a certain pedantry more obstinate than the tape-worm, and for him disastrous, both at the barber's and at the printer's. "You must pull yourself together!" they said to him. "Live and let live," they added. He had no talent for pulling himself together and for living and letting live, in which he found himself more awkward than a seal frying pancakes. . . .
>
> And there was, for him, the problem of ill: the fable of disease, the strange fable spread by the conquistadores, who were enabled to note down the dying words of the Incas. According to them death comes for nothing, suffused in silence, like a tacit, final combination of thought. (pp. 49–50)

Roscioni wrote about Gonzalo: ". . . he is Argentinian and Lombard, a Celtic and a German, a marquis and a bourgeois, an engineer and a writer, a reader of Plato and a peddler of handkerchiefs; he is the Miser, the Misanthrope, the *Malade imaginaire*, the Enemy of the People; he is Eneas and Rodrigo Borgia, . . . a character with an almost unlimited gestual possibility."[16]

In particular, Gonzalo is a character whose *condition humaine* is defined by the author as "a psychopathological grotesque," an obsession deriving "from his exasperated awareness of common beastliness" and from the others' enormous "dissociality"; Gonzalo's neurosis is manifested (to use words by which Gadda refers to him-

---

[16] Gian Carlo Roscioni, "La conclusione della 'Cognizione del dolore,'" *Paragone* 238 (December 1969): 86–99; quoted material is on p. 92.

self in the introduction to the Italian edition, pp. 32 and 37) in the "intolerance, seeming cruelty, 'misanthropic' delays of his thought"; and at the narrative level it is manifested in a love-hatred for his mother, with a related symbolic parricide.

The love-hatred is openly Freudian and should have culminated (in the unfinished part of the novel as well as of "Novella seconda") in the death of the mother. The significance of the relationship between the son and the mother—who are juxtaposed throughout the narrative—is to be found in their different approaches to contingent reality. Gonzalo, in his search for the absolute, cannot but reject the world as it is, "full of sound and fury," and look at it with disgust mixed with compassion. On the contrary, his mother is practical, concrete; like Zeno's wife, Augusta, she is a laborious little ant, and her head does not spin when she thinks of the stars and the earth rotating in the universe: "Many things she had learned and taught: and she knew Kepler's matheses and quadratures that pursue in the senseless vacuity of space the ellipse of our desperate grief" (p. 134). The mother accepts all the limitations, compromises, and illusory values of this world, and above all she accepts the real estate, which in Gadda's polemic becomes the objective correlative of the notion of the self in Western metaphysics: "the Matrix Idea of the villa she had appropriated for herself as a rubescent organ or prime entelechy consubstantial with the womb, and therefore inalienable from the sacred wholeness of her person"; "to that pituitary sum, recondite, noumenical, there corresponded externally—jewel or prime cock crest beyond the confines of the psyche—the objective villa, the datum" (pp. 150–151). Here Gonzalo's polemic against his mother is one with Gadda's written polemic against the bad taste and selfishness of the bourgeoisie, as it is symbolized in the ugly villa built on the lovely melancholic Brianza hills. The psychopathological, the metaphysical, and the sociological are strictly interwoven in Gadda's narrative texture.

Also, Gonzalo's symbolic parricide is recounted on two occasions and seems addressed to his mother rather than his father—as an excruciating indication to her that there are evils and sorrows in the world, that the world is not an absolute value in itself: "He took from the wall a painting, a portrait (as he did also in another excess, years later), and flattened it against the ground. The sheet of glass broke. After which he stepped on it: trampling as if he were pressing grapes in a vat, he reduced the glass to tiny pieces. His heels drew a kind of moustache on the portrait, two frightful bruises on the portrait" (pp. 180–181). The personification of the portrait through the suggestion that it has been bruised seems to express all of Gonzalo's love-hatred and all of Gadda's pietas.

Through Gonzalo's neurosis, Gadda expresses his *vision du monde*, or *referto* as he says, using a medical term in a metaphoric, nontechnical way (as it was in *Anastomòsi*). As the philologist Pietro Pucci points out, this *referto*, grotesque and baroque, is presented with a "vast diagram of expressive modes . . . for the simultaneous representation of the thousand different faces of reality."[17]

Gadda's style is thoroughly based on the "spastic usage" of language in order to obtain "a dissolution-renovation of value" of each noun,[18] as well as on the contributions of the various techniques, the literary and the common language, and the final result is a truly luxuriant vocabulary.[19] This vocabulary, in itself, is a symptom of a sort of linguistic alienation, of a mannerism à la Binswanger, that constitutes both a prologue and a reply to the baroque of the world. Gadda's style produces a "bituminous epos,"[20] a myriad of images

[17] Pietro Pucci, "Lingua e dialetto in Pasolini e in Gadda," *Società* 14, no. 2 (March–April 1958): 381–398; quoted material is on p. 391.

[18] Gadda, "Come lavoro," in *I viaggi la morte*, p. 20. This spastic use of language, suggested by Horace, is again stressed on pp. 84, 97, and especially 169 (apropos of the spoken, popular words of the poet Belli).

[19] On Gadda's vocabulary, at least the following critics should be consulted: Gianfranco Contini, "Saggio introduttivo," in *La cognizione del dolore*, by Gadda, pp. 5–28, "Primo approccio al *Castello di Udine*," in *Esercizi di lettura*, pp. 195–204, and "Carlo Emilio Gadda traduttore espressionista," in *Varianti e altra linguistica*, pp. 303–307; Pietro Citati, "Il male invisibile," in *Il tè del cappellaio matto*, pp. 286–317; and Piero Gelli, "Sul lessico di Gadda," *Paragone* 230 (April 1969): 52–77 (where realistic expressionism is considered as a basic function of Gadda's prose).

[20] Claudio Altarocca, "Gadda, neogaddismo e alcune considerazioni sulla lingua d'uso," *Il Mulino* 19, no. 208 (March–April 1970): 310–322; quoted material is

and scenes all seen in the same perspective (and therefore indicating the meaningless but vital chaos of reality), and a series of
"mirrorlike structures" at the syntactical level that, according to
Arnaldo Ceccaroni's analysis, represent the catalogue of appearances of this reality.[21]

Indeed in Gadda one finds all the elements considered by Auerbach and Lukács as they describe the modern novel: hostility toward contemporary society, fragmentation of reality, and escape
into the psychopathological.

Therefore it will be necessary to examine how Gadda succeeds in
historicizing his *vision du monde*; hints and allusions to a precise
historical and social reality, of course, are not lacking in *La cognizione del dolore, Quer pasticciaccio brutto de via Merulana, L'Adalgisa*, or *I viaggi la morte*. But he has also written a novel-treatise
that makes these hints and allusions explicit and that makes them
the basis for a true personal psychoanalysis of history: *Eros e Priapo
(Da furore a cenere)*. Our critical attention will be focused on this
work instead of the others because it is a clarifying summa of their
motifs.

Gadda's intention in writing *Eros e Priapo* is clearly manifested
from the very beginning: "Evil must be known and notified. And
when it is announced with trumpets from the high mountains, then
and only then the secret mechanism of every sequence will be
known by us and almost seen functioning under the fragile crust of
surface dialectics and the sugar of official bulletins."[22] Indeed Gadda

---

on p. 312: "Epos: the cultivated, learned, rational, Leibnitzian part; bituminous:
the low, popular, dialectal and vitalistic-Bergsonian part."

[21] Arnaldo Ceccaroni, "Per una lettura del 'Pasticciaccio' di Carlo Emilio
Gadda," *Lingua e stile* 5, no. 1 (April 1970): 57–85. The author, by relating
Pasticciaccio to the "detective stories" by Poe and Borges, institutes the equation:
"delinquent: crime = childhood trauma: neurosis," thereby showing the fundamental identity between Ingravallo's inquiry/*quête* and Gonzalo's "cognition of
grief."

[22] Carlo Emilio Gadda, *Eros e Priapo (Da furore a cenere)* (published in 1967
but probably written in 1947, or soon after the Second World War), p. 27. Subsequent references will be to this edition. The notions of erotic charge and narcissism are in other books by Gadda, such as *L'Adalgisa: Disegni milanesi*, p.
153, note 12, and *I viaggi la morte*, p. 21.

wants to arrive at a "cognizance of grief" that he had not been able
to achieve fully through his alter ego, Gonzalo; he wants to give a
name to the obscure invisible evil so that it will become known, in
fact "notified," and visible to all: an individual ill, but even more
a collective one, which Gadda wants to discover and analyze by
utilizing the data and the terms of his very personal psychoanalysis:

> I will have to follow obscure routes. More than the conscious erotic
> states, evident for men, well I intend to pursue the Ariadnean thread of
> the hidden states, not registered and perhaps not even sensed by the dis-
> tinguished dialectics. . . .
>
> Eros is at the roots of the individual life and mind; and it is the source
> of the plural instinct and the social practice of every sociality and de
> facto association, and of every phenomenon that you might call "col-
> lective."
>
> The relationships between "the one" and "the others" are Eros, some-
> times counterfeited, sometimes transfigured and sublimated: and con-
> cealed or spoken. (pp. 29–30)

The result is "an erotic history of human kind" (p. 31), such as
Gaius Suetonius and Publius Tacitus gave us in antiquity when
they described "Nero's dirty and bloody madness, and Tiberius's
dark psychosis" (p. 15). Like these two historians of ancient times,
Gadda is not a psychiatrist, even though he has read "French hand-
books of psychiatry" and Freud since the thirties when they were
prohibited by fascism.[23] But Gadda wants to and knows how to show
the "gangrenous" smell he perceives in the historical and social
phenomena of his times using psychoanalysis as an instrument of
"his attack on the world, of his taking possession of the matter, of
his protective aggressions, of his 'concrete fury' ":[24] "In the false
outcries of a fake life, in the falling down of a history sacrificed to
the vacuum of nothingness, from minute to minute, from sorrow to
sorrow, from anger to anger, from fascist 'ejja' to fascist 'ejja', from
drumbeat to drumbeat, little by little I was reaching my desperate
knowledge" (p. 21). Gadda's language is patterned (in the original,
which cannot but be betrayed by the translation) after the high

[23] Michel David, *La psicoanalisi nella cultura italiana*, p. 458.
[24] Ibid., p. 465.

Latin of the ancient historians and is corrected by the *diminutio* of dialectal and spoken insertions. It immediately reveals the author with his neuroses and idiosyncrasies: we can link Gadda's discourse to Gonzalo's disgust for phenomena, to his painful curiosity for the myriads of manifestations of the real, which all together make up a truly "awful mess." From the beginning it is possible to imagine that Gadda's ambition to write a novel-treatise will be frustrated and that even this work will remain unfinished like the other novels. Toward the end of the book, in fact, one reads, "Now I must schematize my exposition, leaving a more detailed and richer protest for another volume" (p. 153). Though unfinished, *Eros e Priapo* is an exceptional enlargement of Gadda's perspective, of his polemic against the world and society—a polemic that in the preceding works remained veiled by metaphor or was accomplished through an allusion or perhaps even a precise but fleeting hint.[25]

Gadda's "act of knowledge" (as well as that of his alter ego, the character De Madrigal) "has to be rooted in truth" (p. 634); his "truthful pen, though blackened by nasty ink" (p. 119), page by page builds a formidable testimony against fascism, against its vulgarity and stupidity even more than its brutality and violence. On the "tragic and Carnival scene of the world" (p. 205), fascism is taken as a specimen of what Gadda hates in that it does not conform to his ideal absolute. In a recent interview he in fact stated: "You will hear that I am a misanthrope, at bottom this is what they think of me. Please deny it, say it is not true."[26] Gadda's statement means that his apparently misanthropic judgments actually correspond exactly to the historical and social truth on which he focuses so sharply. In this connection he quotes a beautiful sentence by Leopardi as supporting evidence in *Eros e Priapo*: "Usually the good and generous persons are very much hated, because ordinarily

---

[25] Recall, for instance, the metaphoric meaning of the Nistitùo and the deafening bell tolling (of fascist propaganda) or the polemical value of the institution-villa in *La cognizione del dolore*; and in *Quer pasticciaccio brutto de via Merulana*, recall the hints against the hypocrisy of censure and the myth of fascist health, as well as some epithets describing Mussolini.

[26] Cesare Garboli, "Non sono un misantropo," *La fiera letteraria*, August 10, 1967, pp. 8–9.

they are sincere and call things by their names—a fault not for-
given by mankind, which never hates so much those who do evil,
or evil itself, as those who name it" (p. 29).

Gadda's statement, so peremptory and pathetic on a personal
level, finds confirmation on the philosophic and literary plane in
Pucci's recent analysis of *La cognizione del dolore*, which utilizes
Lacan's interpretation of Molière's Alceste to explain the apparently
misanthropic Gonzalo as "an aggressive narcissist" who even at the
end of his tirade against personal pronouns ("the lice of thought")
falls back into his own "I." But, according to Pucci, Gonzalo is also
a moment of a process of awareness about fascism and the worst
aspects of the bourgeois system (with the related sense of impo-
tence, disgust, and death). This moment does not become a "tragic
manifestation of a *conscience malheureuse*," in that Gadda-Gonzalo
takes refuge in "the nonsense of chaos of phenomena, in the sneer-
ing caricature of the thousand faces of Appearance," whereby
"actually tragedy is avoided, unknown to Gonzalo himself, precisely
because of the double prostitution of the phenomenal world, which
succeeds in giving him a help—a maternal help to him who is
desperate—or in being caricatured, thereby becoming a source of
inventions and nominal, literary transformations."[27] After that
extraordinary invention of *Quer pasticciaccio*, certainly *Eros e
Priapo* thoroughly confirms Pucci's thesis, above all explaining the
political and social reasons for Gadda's rancor, not in tragic terms
but through caricature.

It is only logical that at the beginning of this rancor there is
fascism, which Gadda experienced disdainfully, silently: "In its
unconscious and animallike forms, in its lowest and not sublimated
aspects, Eros was dominant on the tragic scene. For twenty years.
. . . A libido, a pictorial and theatrical lust led Italy to sacrifice during those catastrophic twenty years—not a ratio, a νοῦς, an ethical
conscience, a religious spirit. . . . The yardstick for the Eros of the
fascist gang will be a 'usual' Eros, well known to mankind" (pp.
42 and 46). This "usual" Eros is analyzed in the second part of the

[27] Pietro Pucci, "The Obscure Sickness," *Italian Quarterly* 11, no. 42 (Fall
1967): 43–62.

novel, which is more like a treatise than is the first. In it, under the pretense of systematizing a phenomenology of Eros (in chapters or items with such significant titles as "Erotia narcissica o antiero-tia," "Teoria del modello narcissico," "Rapporto fondamentale tra narcisismo e sensualità"), Gadda accomplishes a series of virtuoso digressions embracing almost all fields of experience. For instance, Dante is described as narcissistically proud of the poem "to which the well-known collaborators contributed" (p. 145); or, with reference to the "I" incorporating the model, "in the rituals of positive religions it is possible to eat and swallow the worshiped god, say the Easter lamb" (p. 159); or the recurrence of a theme, already present in *La cognizione del dolore*, which will be examined later: "The self-libido expresses the necessary cohesion of the Self, and is for the single being what centripetal force or gravity is for the single planet. It is identified with the pronoun I" (pp. 145–146).[28]

But the erotic history of mankind is above all developed as an erotic history of fascism and especially of the leader who embodied it. Benito Mussolini is the focus of the first fifty pages of the novel, which then, by becoming almost a treatise, seems to testify to the completion of a revenge carried out by the author with "lucid anger" (p. 185)—"from fury to ashes," as the subtitle of the novel puts it with a reference also to the end of fascism's twenty years. Here is the figure of Mussolini in Gadda's carnival representation:

He arrived at making a few panting janitors run at his pressing a button—the highest dream of the former Socialist agitator. He arrived at the gaiters of the turtle-dove color, which he used to wear with the ease of an orangutan; at the ruled trousers, the morning coat, the white gloves typical of a *commendatore* or a uricacidemic stock-exchange broker, hated but lividly envied bourgeois. His hands were like big banana bunches, hanging beside his hips and held by short, short arms. . . . He arrived at the plume of the emir, of the leader of square legions in precipitous retreat. (Not their fault, poor dead—poor living!) On his belly, at the large belt, a knife: the symbol and even more the obscene instrument of the brawl. (p. 18)

The caricature by far transcends the physical aspects of Mussolini

[28] Cf. Gadda, *Acquainted with Grief*, pp. 86–89.

and is thoroughly imbued with morality and elegy. Gadda's fury finds a particular outlet in the metaphorical transposition (It is some metaphor!) of a speech by Mussolini from the balcony of Palazzo Venezia in Rome:

Then the reiterated exultation of the whole body, as if a spring were throwing it upward—of the whole abundant person: in order to seem an even greater emir on top of four hoofs; then the sudden protuberance of that phallic proboscis of his, snoutlike in the dimension of a swine. . . . "ecco ecco ecco eja eja eja," the glorious and virile excitement of the no-longer-seen masturbation: and the consequent virile pollution in the face of the many, of the clapping. . . . And the Alps and the Apennines were echoing him, hì-hà, hì-hà, re-echoing him ad infinitum, hè-jà, hè-jà, through the infinite design of the valleys (and of Foscolo's dales). (pp. 37–38)

It is to be noted that the reference to Ugo Foscolo has a definite purpose. In an extraordinary three-voice dialogue entitled *Il guerriero, l'amazzone, lo spirito della poesia nel verso immortale del Foscolo*, Gadda reproaches the romantic poet for the same Priapean narcissism of Mussolini (and Napoleon Bonaparte), the same virile exaltation, the same false rhetoric, in other words the same erotic states "disguised as noble appearances, or concocted in the sauces of glory, or tied to beautiful names, to high-sounding words, to 'magnanimous senses' " (p. 29): "In Ugo Foscolo I don't hate the poet: if anything, I hate the histrionic," says De' Linguagi in the dialogue, as the spokesman for Gadda.[29]

However, Mussolini by himself did not exhaust fascism; uniforms, crowds, parades, youth, women are other elements of fascism that Gadda examines one by one, pitilessly. The ecstatic crowds acclaiming the "Duce" or repeating his words in a monkeylike fashion while distorting them in sexual meanings or exploding in the fascist outcry, which is nothing but a solemn collective bray, are particular objects of Gadda's harsh representation. By contrast, one is reminded of the simple and very effective way in which Ignazio Silone characterized the senselessness of the so-called

---

[29] In *Paragone* 116 (August 1959): 43–77. Also, in "San Giorgio in casa Brocchi" Gadda demystifies Cicero.

Oceanic rallies in *Fontamara*: the crowd's cry is exactly tran-
scribed, but out of phase by one syllable—CEDU! CEDU![30] In addition to the crowds, the fascist hierarchs with their boots, the political
threshings, the city blackouts (do you remember Calvino's "Le notti
dell'UNPA"?), and the war widows fall under Gadda's polemical
pen. This pen is particularly pointed against women, and the author's misogyny is revealed in passages of extreme ferocity, like
the following, which presupposes the equestrian image of Mussolini:

A woman loves and dreams of the mounted soldier, the mounted colonel,
the mounted lieutenant, and the horseman: for her the spurs cruelly
suggest that inexorable pressure exercised by the male on her while in-
quiring her mystery and compelling her delicate unwillingness to pleasure. . . . A lance or a sword then, useless to say, proposes the best verb to
her. That is, the verb "to pierce." And that prancing and going up and
down of the loins, the trunk, the neck, in the cinematic alternation
caused by trot are the symbol or the image of another riding and pro-
gressing, in another much desired alternation. (pp. 53–54)

It might be worth recalling that Goffredo Parise, in a different
context in his dialogue *L'assoluto naturale,* also gives vent to the
acrimony he feels against women. He portrays them almost as a
species in themselves, inimical to men in a Darwinian way, ready
perhaps to inflict (or to be subjected to) "a total devouring."[31] This
is indeed the woman-insect (the latest expression of the "Praying
Mantis" made famous by Mario Praz) in her scenographic costumes
that are designed to make her appear "a flower, then a dragonfly, a
butterfly, anyway always belonging to flora and fauna."[32] Woman's
feminine practicality, physiological concreteness, and social solidity
are juxtaposed to the idealistic man, poet and thinker: it is she who
wants man to be bourgeois, so much so that to demonstrate her in-
satiability an entire scene of the dialogue is literally flooded with

[30] It is necessary, however, to recall above all Ignazio Silone's *La scuola dei
dittatori*, a civil and painful denunciation of fascism and nazism. Gadda's pages
on the psychology of crowds are directly related to Freud's *Psychology of the
Masses and Analysis of the Self*.

[31] Goffredo Parise, *L'assoluto naturale*, p. 38.

[32] Ibid., p. 9.

objects bought by her. In sum, for Parise woman is juxtaposed to man as nature is juxtaposed to history, matter to spirit, reality to imagination.

Something similar is found in Gadda when he states, "In general, women do not create the future: they perfect the past, with a more or less marked delay, as opposed to the results of male avant garde" (p. 56). Later he describes the manifestations of narcissistic possession of objects as being acritical, inauthentic, and, above all, precisely characteristic of women. In such descriptions Gadda's imagination is regulated on an immediate level by "clearly sexuophobic filters"[33] that point to his fundamental Oedipal complex; he indulges in a series of inventions that in the end are disdainful insults (expressed in sexual terms) against appearance: one remembers the page on the elegant bag, which Gadda considers almost an epitome of bourgeois ladies and which he, with a neologism, calls a "pussybag" (*ficoborsa*);[34] or his explicit recourse to the idea-Villa as a particular case of the (no longer fascist but bourgeois) phenomenon already treated and here taken up again to confirm his assertions: "Also in *La cognizione del dolore* D. M. spoke of 'narcissistic consubstantiation': today he would say narcissistic hyperbole, erroneous emphasizing of non-being; in fact it is impossible to emphasize what does not exist. At that time he was speaking of a lady owner and of the emphasized object of her possession, which was a poor house" (p. 126). Apropos of this lady owner, who was Gonzalo's mother, we remember "the Matrix-Idea of the villa she had appropriated for herself as a rubescent organ or prime entelechy consubstantial with the womb, and therefore inalienable

[33] Enzo Golino, "Con Priapo a Palazzo Venezia," *L'espresso*, August 13, 1967, p. 19.

[34] Gadda, *Eros e Priapo*, p. 127: "In the leather bag, called handbag but actually big bag for the kind ladies, we can distinguish (when we are allowed by our impudence and foolishness) the 'labia majora': inside, when you open them, you can perceive the 'labia minora' with an interior latch-clitoris: deeper inside there is an intimate small bag and inside this small bag a purse, with various sections, almost the heart's ventricles and auricles of a child about to be born." Cf. Gadda, *L'Adalgisa: Disegni milanesi*, p. 277, note 25: "The handbag or bag or large bag, now (1943) sexual organ for the elegant or para-elegant strata of the population, in those times did not exist."

from the sacred wholeness of her person."[35] The recourse in the context of the treatise on Eros helps to characterize and historicize the contrast between Gonzalo and his mother, a contrast that is ideologic-metaphysical even more than Oedipal in that the longing for an absolute is juxtaposed to the acceptance of the contingent, the phenomenal.[36] But of course Gadda, in recalling *La cognizione del dolore*, inserts his literary biography in the context of his erotic phenomenology, thus actually transforming it into a "bewitching and bitter autobiographic parade."[37]

At this point the Lacanian and dialectical interpretation given by Pucci is most convincingly confirmed: in fact Gadda, on his part, does not at all give up that narcissism he bitterly denounces in the fascist aberrations, in the others' dissociality.

If in Mussolini, Eros not guided by Logos becomes Priapus, on the contrary in Gadda, Eros inspired by Logos becomes the sponsor of a highly civic enterprise, the act of knowledge and denunciation of evil. But obviously Gadda's Eros could not be content with this; already in the preceding analysis we have seen how many times his "I" peeps in on the narration (from misogyny to autobiography). Gadda's Eros is actually disguised as Logos; it becomes Logos. After all, we are talking about a book by Gadda, and in erotic phenomenology a book has a well-defined meaning:

Generally, exhibition is the fundamental act of narcissistic psychosis. The transposition of the prime exhibiting act into another exhibiting act with a sublimated content is determined by a process that is symbolic and analogical. . . . You have substituted the exhibition of the good work for that of your person: this work is the unconscious symbol of the other, and to publish it is an operation "analogous" to publicizing the person. I do not insist. The sublimation of the elementary narcissistic act is an evident function in the biography of individual persons as well as in the history of peoples. (pp. 202–203)

With these statements on the transposition of the prime exhibiting

[35] Gadda, *Acquainted with Grief*, p. 150.

[36] Cf. Pucci, "The Obscure Sickness," pp. 58–62.

[37] Geno Pampaloni, "Quando cala il voltaggio," *La fiera letteraria*, August 31, 1967, p. 19.

act and on the psychic mechanism of the symbolic or analogical function, Gadda seems to anticipate some of the directions of research of the *École freudienne de Paris* concerning precisely "un mécanisme identique d'oscillation métaphoro-métonymique" through which art represents a sublimation of the erotic force and is inserted in a well-defined structure of the psyche.[38]

As for Gadda, he certainly carries out the exhibitionistic act of writing and of publishing in order to be recognized. He writes *Eros e Priapo* in the first person; then, using brief incidental and parenthetical insertions (such as "De Madrigal says," or "De Madrigal continued"), he almost surreptitiously introduces his alter ego, De Madrigal, with his airy and mocking name, as a mirror of himself and of what he is saying. In the end he acquaints the readers with his autobiography by means of his character, who is central in the final pages of the book, especially in the *discours indirect libre* and sometimes also in direct speech, as in the following example:

My schoolfellow Alì Oco De Madrigal has told me he had as narcissistic models the Black Corsair, Dante (for a long time), the famous Ariosto, still for a long time, Julius Caesar, Nicholas Deck (a Wallachian hunter-peasant, a character in Jules Verne's *Le Château des Carpathes*), Count Franz von Telèk (in the same story), Shakespeare; later Cervantes, the greatest of European inventors, maimed at Lepanto. You will say, "Well, these models have really done it for your poor Alì Oco, in order for him to be that fool he obviously is." Granted the fool. But he went on: "Generally, I am fascinated by distinction, be it that of the ancient Spanish cultural maceration, of Caravaggio's painting, of Spanish theologians and theological works, of thin and tall persons: I would rather be Don Quixote or Ignacio de Loyola than a poor sacristan." (p. 161)

The reference to Don Quixote points peremptorily to Gonzalo in *La cognizione del dolore*, who is precisely a hidalgo, always fighting the windmills of appearance, and a fool who, pathetically, "makes a confusion that is full of sense: he attacks the weak defenses of phe-

---

[38] Guy Rosolato, "Etude des perversions sexuelles à partir du fétichisme," in *Le désir et la perversion*, p. 38.

nomena with metaphysical fury, with the tearing force of truth; he pursues, destroys, reduces them to pieces."[39]

But in *Eros e Priapo* De Madrigal is more than Gadda's spokesman. Let us remember the author's taste for the phantasmagory of language, verbal manipulations, noun transformations, and puns; a few random examples will suffice: Mussolini's "phallic dogma or dogmatic fallacy," and the untranslatable puns "Culiseo" and "*era favista*" (instead of "Colosseo" and "*era fascista*"); the comparison between Alexander the Great who arrived at Alexandria of Egypt "*col cocchio*" and Mussolini who arrived "*col cacchio*" (that is, he never arrived there at all); the incredible sequel of epithets and attributes he applies to the dictator, from "Bombetta" to "Mascellone"—just as Foscolo was "Basetta" and Napoleon a "dwarf," a "meagerly proud smallness."[40] At this point it will not be surprising to discover that De Madrigal is not as much a character, an alter ego for Gadda as were Gonzalo and Ingravallo, as he is a pretext, a verbal play, a noun transformation, literally an anagram:

ALI' OCO DE MADRIGAL;

if we break it down and then reassemble it letter by letter, it becomes

CARLO EMILIO GADDA.

This is a good example indeed, in the context of the novel-treatise, of Eros become Logos, with a wink to the reader and a scoff to "toothless eternity."[41]

The last quotation refers back to the pole that opposes history, that is, the absolute. Returning to *La cognizione del dolore*, where an understanding of the longing for the absolute is fundamental to an

[39] Pucci, "The Obscure Sickness," p. 58.

[40] The definitions of Foscolo and Napoleon are in the cited dialogue, pp. 46–47, and in Gadda's *La cognizione del dolore*, pp. 32–33; the description of Napoleon's crowning in Milan is in Gadda's *L'Adalgisa*, p. 50; the epithet Mascellone for Mussolini is to be found, along with others, in *Quer pasticciaccio brutto de via Merulana*.

[41] Gadda, *Eros e Priapo*, p. 39. Cf. Gadda, *L'Adalgisa*, pp. 175–176: "It was the tavern of the moment: they were drinking the moment. The old Eternity, grimacing, let them debauch."

understanding of the protagonist Gonzalo, one notices that, just as evil is not only physical, it is not only in history. At the end of a conscientious medical checkup (the doctor is the embodiment of the naturalistic level to be transcended in the reading), Gonzalo emblematically puts the prescription under "a polished little polyhedron of ground crystal, all glints. He seemed . . . to have forgotten the sickness—'*le mal physique*,' in this case: the visible sickness" (p. 69). What matters is the invisible sickness uncovered by Gadda's diagnosis:

An unpious sentiment, one would have said a deep and very remote rancor, had been swelling in the spirit of the son. . . . This sorrowful perturbation, stronger than any moderating entreaty of the will, seemed to come out on occasions and on pretexts from a deep, inexpiable zone of shrouded verities: from a torment without confession.

It was the obscure sickness of which histories and laws and the universal disciplines of the great chairs persist in having to ignore the causes, the stages; and one bears it within himself along all the resplendent descent of a lifetime, heavier every day, without medication. (p. 187)

Here sickness for Gadda seems indeed to be the ontological foundation of life.[42] The "misanthropic" Gonzalo seems to take the burden of this sickness upon himself, as an expiation for, or a liberation from, a contingent reality that prevents absolute knowledge:

To seize the lying kiss of Appearance, to lie with her on the straw, to breathe her breath, to drink in, down into the soul, her belch and strumpet's stench. Or instead to plunge them into rancor and into contempt as into a well of excrement, to deny, to deny. . . .

The hidalgo, perhaps, meant to negate himself: claiming for himself the motives of grief, the acquaintance with grief and the truth of it; nothing was left to possibility. Everything was exhausted by the theft of grief. Only the contempt for designs and appearances was safe, that tragic mask on the metope of the theater. (p. 171)

Gonzalo pursues his stubborn and exhaustive cognition of or ac-

[42] See Guido Guglielmi, *Letteratura come sistema e come funzione*, p. 133: "The *invisible evil* is nothing more than a semantic archaism," which is placed in "a dissonant relationship with the normal norm of the language."

quaintance with grief exactly as the surgeon in *Anastomòsi* proceeded with the point of his unperturbed knowledge. At all levels, for Gadda it is a cognitive operation.

At any rate, *La cognizione del dolore* has an inner development similar to Svevo's and Michelstaedter's, with a desperate lyricism that harkens back to Leopardi (and therefore to Schopenhauer) and an emphasis on psychopathology that is not an end in itself but rather expresses a precise and compassionate *referto* on the human condition. Furthermore, Gadda is able to deal with the most directly literary aspect of his *vision du monde*. He does so, significantly, by representing Gonzalo speaking to his doctor, who does not understand his outburst of rage directed initially and not by chance against the pronoun "I" ("the foulest of all pronouns").

> *"Je pense* true *mais j'en ai marre de penser"* [in the original text: "I think; *già:* but I'm ill of thinking"], the son murmured. "Pronouns! They're the lice of thought! When a thought has lice, it scratches, like everyone who has lice . . . and they get in the fingernails, then . . . you find pronouns, the personal pronouns. . . .
>
> "The mere fact that we go on proclaiming 'I, you' with uncouth mouths . . . with our avarice of the constipated, predestined to putrescence, I, you—this very fact, I, you—reveals the baseness of common dialectics . . . and guarantees our impotence in preaching anything about anything . . . since we are ignorant of . . . the subject of every possible proposition." (pp. 86–87)

And again, in a term of rage mixed with self-irony:

> When Being becomes separated into a sack of foul guts, whose boundaries are more miserable and more foolish than this foolish, taxpaying wall . . . which you can climb over in one leap . . . when this fine business happens . . . then . . . that's when the I is determined, with its fine monad upon it, like the caper on the rolled-up anchovy on the lemon slice over the Wiener schnitzel. Then, then! That precisely is the very moment! That lousy, incomparable I . . . swaggering . . . erect . . . beplumed with attributes of every sort . . . purplish, and feathered, and taut, and turgid . . . like a turkey . . . in an open fantail of engineering diplomas, of noble titles . . . (p. 89)

Gonzalo's outburst is beautiful from a rhetorical standpoint: the cogent and panting pauses, the aphorism of lice, the mannerist stratification in the comparison involving the caper (in assonance with monad), and in the Italian original the final rhyme "ingegne-reschi/cavallereschi." But the importance of this outburst is in the fact that it is the narrative climax of Gadda's discourse that started with the organic tangle in *Anastomòsi* ("a heap of flaccid tripes"—here "a sack of foul guts" with "miserable" boundaries) and developed in the excerpts quoted from "Come lavoro" and *Eros e Priapo*. This discourse is not so much on metaphysics as it is against metaphysics, and as such it should be considered in a wide cultural context. Taking Nietzsche as a starting point, then psycho-analysis (and particularly Georg Groddeck),[43] one remembers Michelstaedter's considerations on "the words of fog," the subjunc-tive, the introductory particles of speech; and, along the same inter-pretive line, one recalls Derrida's contemporary statements that seem to frame Svevo's analogous intuitions philosophically.

Gadda's polemic against the pronouns emerges as a part of a much larger cognitive polemic. His considerations on history and literature are fundamental on this point:

Our words—you'll allow me—are everyone's words, very much pub-lished ones, handed down to us by peoples and doctrines. . . . Our phrases, our words are moments-pauses (the waiting landings, so to speak) of a cognitive-expressive flow (or ascent). . . . Their history, which is the crazy history of man, illustrates the meanings of each of them: four, or twelve, or twenty-three; the nuances, the minimal variations in value; in other terms, their semantic difference.

A writer's technique, to a certain extent, grows out of a pre-individual background that is the common adoption of language, that is the se-mantic stock (bearer of meanings) of a history-experience already real-ized and consolidated. This stock is formed and articulated through ac-

[43] Georg Groddeck, *Psychoanalytische Schriften zur Psychosomatik*, p. 266: "Language is a drawback for civilization. Think about it! Language has a word, I, which resounds everywhere, penetrates into and dominates our whole life. . . . However, no I exists, and when we say, I think, I live, this is a lie, a misrepre-sentation. We should say, it thinks, it lives (*Es denkt, Es lebt*). The Id: the great mystery of the world. An I does not exist." Also, cf. the chapter on the nature of pronouns in Émile Benveniste, *Problèmes de linguistique générale*, pp. 251–257.

ceptance or antithesis, by enrichment or negation of certain expressive
modes. The adoption of a language should be referred to a collective
work, historically capitalized in an idiomatic mass, historically conse-
quential in a certain development or more generally in some sort of deformation. In sum, this experience goes beyond the boundaries of a
single personality and allows us to think of a history of poetry in a collective sense.[44]

These remarks could be compared with T. S. Eliot's "Tradition
and the Individual Talent"; in any case, they illuminate "the expressive contributions of techniques" in Gadda's work. *Anastomòsi*
is a particularly meaningful example of the effective use of the
terminology of surgical technique, but in Gadda's pages one finds
the "idiomatic masses" elaborated "in the different technical milieux" listed by the author as follows: "factories, army, navy, arts
and professions, commerce, official bulletins, sciences, fashion,
underworld, medicine and clinics and insane asylums, stock-
exchange, business, clothing, journalism, police, bureaucracy, law,
agriculture, rackets."[45]

Gadda's considerations on words, however, go beyond a purely
stylistic problem. On the one hand, they correspond to the latest
results of structural linguistics; on the other, they could be appropriated by Raimondi in *Metafora e storia* (metaphor and history,
with metaphor incorporating history and in turn being created by
the latter).

But another point is worthy of examination. After having po-
litely asserted that there is "some exactness" in his "modest
thought" that a writer should be a bit "the Encyclopedia," Gadda
fully realizes that the encyclopedic project is impossible. The catalogue of the appearances of reality, the linguistic and stylistic ac-
cumulation and variation ("*singula enumerare*" and "*omnia cir-
cumspicere,*" as Roscioni puts it) never exhaust totality.[46] That is
why the encyclopedia cannot be completed, the book must remain

---

[44] Gadda, *I viaggi la morte*, pp. 19–20 and 77–78.

[45] Ibid., p. 81.

[46] Ibid., and Gian Carlo Roscioni, *La disarmonia prestabilita: Studio su Gadda*,
pp. 31, 63.

open, writing does not exhaust the word: "One must actually look at the world, in order to be able to represent it; so, by looking at it, one happens to note that to a certain extent the world has already represented itself: already, before the poet, the soldier has spoken of the battle, and the sailor of the sea, and the woman-in-childbed of her delivery."[47]

Gadda's writing, then, only appears to be representative and is necessarily unfinished; in Jacqueline Risset's words, it continuously searches for "the point that prevents the closing, . . . the indefinite crossing of plans that always sends *forward*, toward the unspeakable point from where it is born in the midst of disorder."[48]

Even in the minimal (but not secondary) example of *Anastomòsi*, in the context of a thematic-symbolic analysis, it is possible to find the unspeakable point from which Gadda's whole writing originated: it is the primordial disorder, the organic tangle, the biological "darkness of the body" to be cut under the light by a "sharp, shining pen." Through the chain surgeon/whiteness/mother, the metaphor of the pen leads to that emblematic image in which it seems that the heuristic germ of Gadda's representation is concentrated: it is precisely that Mother, constituting the term *ad quem*, from which continuously, without ever being able to be concluded, his writing is born.

[47] Gadda, *I viaggi la morte*, p. 91.
[48] Jacqueline Risset, "Carlo Emilio Gadda ou La philosophie à l'envers," *Critique* 282 (November 1970): 944–951; quoted material is on p. 951.

BIBLIOGRAPHY

Almansi, Guido. "La bassa voglia: Divagazioni sulla 'volgarità' dell'arte." *Il Ponte* 27, no. 4 (April 1971): 491–503. Now in *L'estetica dell'osceno*, pp. 195–211. Turin: Einaudi, 1974.

———. "Il tema dell'incesto in Italo Svevo." *Paragone*, no. 264 (February 1972), pp. 47–60.

Alonge, Roberto. *Pirandello tra realismo e mistificazione.* Naples: Guida, 1972.

Altarocca, Claudio. "Gadda, neogaddismo e alcune considerazioni sulla lingua d'uso." *Il Mulino* 19, no. 208 (March–April 1970): 310–322.

Alvaro, Corrado. *See* Pirandello, Luigi.

Arcangeli, Francesco. *Dal Romanticismo all'informale.* Bologna: Università di Bologna, 1971.

Artaud, Antonin. *Oeuvres complètes.* Paris: Gallimard, 1956.

Asor Rosa, Alberto. *Thomas Mann o dell'ambiguità borghese.* Bari: De Donato, 1971.

Astaldi, Maria Luisa. *Nascita e vicende del romanzo italiano.* Milan: Treves, 1939.

Auerbach, Erich. *Mimesis: The Representation of Reality in Western Literature.* Translated by Willard R. Trask. New York: Doubleday Anchor, 1957.

Bakan, David. *Disease, Pain and Sacrifice.* Chicago: University of Chicago Press, 1968.

Baldi, Guido. *Carlo Emilio Gadda.* Milan: Mursia, 1972.

Bàrberi Squarotti, Giorgio. *Il codice di Babele.* Milan: Rizzoli, 1972.

Barilli, Renato. *La barriera del naturalismo.* Milan: Mursia, 1964.

———. *La linea Svevo-Pirandello.* Milan: Mursia, 1972.

Basaglia, Franco. *L'istituzione negata.* Turin: Einaudi, 1968.

———. *La maggioranza deviante.* Turin: Einaudi, 1971.

Bassani, Giorgio. *Le parole preparate.* Turin: Einaudi, 1966.

Baxandall, Lee, ed. *Radical Perspective on the Arts.* Harmondsworth: Penguin, 1972.

Bazlen, Roberto. *Lettere editoriali.* Milan: Adelphi, 1968.

Béguin, Albert. *Le Romantisme Allemand.* Ligugé: Les Cahiers du Sud, 1949.

Béhar, Henri. *L'univers médical de Proust.* Paris: Gallimard, 1971.

Benjamin, Walter. *Illuminations.* Translated by Harry Zohn. New York: Schocken, 1969.

Benveniste, Émile. *Problèmes de linguistique générale.* Paris: Gallimard, 1966.

Berardi, Gianluigi. "Mito dei primitivi e coerenza storica in *Tigre Reale.*" In *Studi letterari per il 250° anniversario della nascita di Carlo Goldoni.* Studia Ghisleriana 2, no. 2. Pavia: Tipografia del libro, 1957.

Berger, Peter L., and Thomas Luckmann. *The Social Construction of Reality: A Treatise in the Sociology of Knowledge.* New York: Doubleday, 1966.

Bersani, Leo. *Balzac to Beckett: Center and Circumference in French Fiction.* New York: Oxford, 1970.

Biasin, Gian-Paolo. "Documenti per Svevo: Dal diario di Elio Schmitz." *MLN* 83, no. 1 (January 1968): 107–125.

Binswanger, Ludwig. *Drei Formen Missglückten Daseins.* Tübingen: Niemeyer, 1956. Italian translation, *Tre forme di esistenza mancata.* Milan: Il Saggiatore, 1964.

———. *Grundformen und Erkenntnis menschlichen Daseins.* Zürich: Niehan, 1942 and 1953.

———. *Heinrich Ibsen und das Problem der Selbstrealisation in der Kunst.* Heidelberg: Schneider, 1949.

———. *Schizophrenie.* Pfullingen: Neske, 1957.

Bo, Carlo. *L'eredità di Leopardi e altri saggi.* Florence: Vallecchi, 1964.

Bonadeo, Alfredo. "Ideale e reale nella *Coscienza di Zeno.*" *Italica* 46, no. 4 (Winter 1969): 402–418.

Bontempelli, Massimo. *Introduzioni e discorsi.* 4th ed. Milan: Bompiani, 1945.

Bouissy, André. "Les fondements idéologiques de l'oeuvre d'Italo Svevo." *Revue des études italiennes* 12, nos. 3–4 (1966): 209–245 and 350–373; 13, no. 1 (1967): 23–50.

Brennan, Donald G., ed. *Arms Control, Disarmament and National Security.* New York: Braziller, 1960.

Calvino, Italo. *I nostri antenati.* Turin: Einaudi, 1960.

Cambon, Glauco. "Zeno come anti-Faust." *Il Verri* 11 (December 1963): 69–76.

————, ed. *Pirandello.* Englewood Cliffs: Prentice-Hall, 1967.

Canguilhem, Georges. *Essai sur quelques problèmes concernant le normal et le pathologique.* Paris: Les Belles Lettres, 1950.

————. *Sain et pathologique.* Paris: P.U.F., 1940.

Cappellani, Nino. *Vita di Giovanni Verga.* Florence: Le Monnier, 1940.

Carter, A. E. *The Idea of Decadence in French Literature, 1830–1900.* Toronto: University of Toronto Press, 1950.

Caruso, Paolo, ed. *Conversazioni con Lévi-Strauss, Foucault, Lacan.* Milan: Mursia, 1969.

Cattaneo, Giulio. *Esperienze intellettuali del primo Novecento.* Milan: Ricciardi, 1968.

————. *Giovanni Verga.* Turin: UTET, 1963.

Caute, David. *The Illusion: An Essay on Politics, Theatre and the Novel.* New York: Harper & Row, 1971.

Ceccaroni, Arnaldo. "Per una lettura del 'Pasticciaccio' di Carlo Emilio Gadda." *Lingua e stile* 5, no. 1 (April 1970): 57–85.

Cecchetti, Giovanni. "Beneath Pirandello's *Naked Masks.*" *Forum Italicum* 1, no. 4 (December 1967): 244–258.

Cecchi, Emilio, and Natalino Sapegno, eds. *Il Novecento,* vol. 9 of *Storia della letteratura italiana.* Milan: Garzanti, 1969.

Ceronetti, Guido. "È ancora possibile scrivere versi galanti?" *L'espresso,* September 19, 1971, p. 11.

Cerruti, Marco. *Carlo Michelstaedter.* Milan: Mursia, 1967.

Chandler, S. B. "The Movement of Life in Verga." *Italica* 35, no. 2 (June 1958): 91–100.

Charlton, Donald G. *Positivist Thought in France during the Second Empire, 1852–1870.* Oxford: Clarendon Press, 1959.

Cherubini, Arnaldo. "La malattia nella 'Scapigliatura.' " *La Serpe* 15, no. 3 (1966): 129–136.

————. "La malattia nel Verismo italiano: La poesia." *La Serpe* 15, no. 15 (1967): 161–169.

————. "La malattia nel Verismo italiano: La prosa." *La Serpe* 15, no. 16 (1967): 97–106.

Citati, Pietro. *Il tè del cappellaio matto.* Milan: Mondadori, 1972.

Contini, Gianfranco. *Esercizi di lettura.* Florence: Le Monnier, 1947.

————. "Saggio introduttivo." In *La cognizione del dolore,* by Carlo Emilio Gadda. Turin: Einaudi, 1969.

————. *Varianti e altra linguistica.* Milan and Naples: Ricciardi, 1970.

Contorbia, Franco. *See* Gozzano, Guido.

Corti, Maria, and Cesare Segre, eds. *I metodi attuali della critica in Italia.* Turin: ERI, 1970.

Curi, Fausto. *Metodo Storia Strutture.* Turin: Paravia, 1971.

Curtius, Ernst Robert. *European Literature and the Latin Middle Ages*. Translated by Willard R. Trask. New York: Pantheon, 1953.

D'Annunzio, Gabriele. *Le novelle della Pescara*. Milan: Oscar Mondadori, 1969.

———. *Prose di ricerca, di lotta, etc.* 4th ed. Milan: Mondadori, 1968.

David, Michel. "La critica psicanalitica." In *I metodi attuali della critica in Italia*, edited by Maria Corti and Cesare Segre. Turin: ERI, 1970.

———. *Letteratura e psicanalisi*. Milan: Mursia, 1967.

———. *La psicoanalisi nella cultura italiana*. Turin: Boringhieri, 1965.

Debenedetti, Giacomo. *Il romanzo del Novecento*. Milan: Garzanti, 1971.

———. *Saggi critici, nuova serie*. Milan: Mondadori, 1945 and 1955.

———. *Saggi critici, prima serie*. Milan: Il Saggiatore, 1969.

———. *Saggi critici, terza serie*. Milan: Il Saggiatore, 1959.

Deleito y Piñuela, José. *El sentimiento de tristeza en la literatura contemporánea*. Barcelona: Minerva, 1922.

Deleuze, Gilles, and Félix Guattari. *L'Anti-Oedipe: Capitalisme et schizophrénie*. Paris: Minuit, 1972.

Del Ministro, Maurizio. "Interpretazione di 'Enrico IV.'" *La Rassegna della letteratura italiana* 75, no. 1 (1969): 16–26.

De Man, Paul. *Blindness and Insight: Essays in the Rhetoric of Contemporary Criticism*. New York: Oxford, 1971.

De Meijer, Pieter. "La Sicilia fra mito e storia nei romanzi del Verga." *La Rassegna della letteratura italiana* 67, no. 1 (January–April 1963): 116–123.

De Roberto, Federico. *Casa Verga e altri saggi verghiani*. Florence: Le Monnier, 1964.

Derrida, Jacques. "La 'différance.'" In *Théorie d'ensemble*. Paris: Seuil, 1968.

———. *La dissémination*. Paris: Seuil, 1972.

———. *L'écriture et la différence*. Paris: Seuil, 1967.

———. *De la grammatologie*. Paris: Minuit, 1967.

———. "Le livre ouvert." Lecture given at Berlin and State University of New York, Buffalo. Fall 1969.

Di Pietro, Antonio. *Luigi Pirandello*. 2d ed. Milan: Vita e Pensiero, 1950.

Donato, Eugenio. *See* Macksey, Richard A.

Eco, Umberto. *La struttura assente: Introduzione alla ricerca semiologica*. Milan: Bompiani, 1968.

Ellenberger, Henri F. *The Discovery of the Unconscious: The History and Evolution of Dynamic Psychiatry*. New York: Basic Books, 1970.

Eruli, Brunella. "Marinetti, quale avanguardia?" *Il Ponte* 25, no. 10 (October 1969): 1303–1316.

Fabbri, Diego. "Pirandello ieri oggi domani." *La fiera letteraria* 42, no. 30 (November 1967): 15–20. A round table with Alberto Moravia, Guido Piovene, Edoardo Sanguineti, Luigi Squarzina, and Manlio Cancogni.

La fabbrica della follia. Edited by Associazione per la lotta contro le malattie mentali. Turin: Einaudi, 1971.

Flaubert, Gustave. *Oeuvres.* 2 vols. Paris: P.U.F., 1951.

Flora, Francesco. "Il decadentismo." In *Questioni e correnti di storia letteraria,* edited by Attilio Momigliano, pp. 761–810. Milan: Marzorati, 1949.

Foucault, Michel. *Madness and Civilization: A History of Insanity in the Age of Reason.* Translated by Richard Howard. New York: Pantheon, 1965.

———. *Maladie mentale et psychologie.* Paris: P.U.F., 1960.

———. *Naissance de la clinique: Une archéologie du regard médical.* Paris: P.U.F., 1963.

———. *The Order of Things: An Archeology of the Human Sciences.* New York: Pantheon, 1970.

Freccero, John. "Zeno's Last Cigarette." *MLN* 77, no. 1 (January 1962): 3–23.

Freud, Sigmund. *Therapy and Technique.* Edited by Philip Reiff. New York: Collier Books, 1963.

———. *Totem and Taboo.* Translated by A. A. Brill. New York: Vintage, n.d.

Friedell, Egon. *Aphorismen und Briefe.* Munich: Beck, 1962.

Furbank, Philip N. *Italo Svevo: The Man and the Writer.* Berkeley: University of California Press, 1966.

Furst, Lilian R. "Italo Svevo's *La coscienza di Zeno* and Thomas Mann's *Der Zauberberg.*" *Contemporary Literature* 9, no. 4 (Fall 1968): 492–506.

Fusco, Mario. *Italo Svevo: Conscience et réalité.* Paris: Gallimard, 1973.

Gadda, Carlo Emilio. *Acquainted with Grief.* Translated by William Weaver. New York: Braziller, 1969.

———. *L'Adalgisa: Disegni milanesi.* Turin: Einaudi, 1963.

———. *La cognizione del dolore.* Turin: Einaudi, 1969.

———. *Eros e Priapo (Da furore a cenere).* Milan: Garzanti, 1967.

———. *I viaggi la morte.* Milan: Garzanti, 1958.

———. *Le meraviglie d'Italia: Gli anni.* Turin: Einaudi, 1964.

———. *Novella seconda.* Milan: Garzanti, 1971.

———. *That Awful Mess on Via Merulana.* Translated by William Weaver. New York: Braziller, 1965.

Garboli, Cesare. "Non sono un misantropo." *La fiera letteraria*, August 10, 1967, pp. 8–9.

Garin, Eugenio. "Omaggio a Carlo Michelstaedter." *Studi goriziani* 24 (July–December 1958): 23–31.

Gelley, Alexander. "Form as Force." *Diacritics* 2, no. 1 (Spring 1972): 9–13.

Gelli, Piero. "Sul lessico di Gadda." *Paragone*, no. 230 (April 1969), pp. 52–77.

Ghidetti, Enrico. *Tarchetti e la Scapigliatura lombarda*. Naples: Libreria Scientifica Editrice, 1968.

Giachery, Emerico. *Verga e D'Annunzio*. Milan: Silva, 1968.

Girard, René. *Deceit, Desire, and the Novel: Self and Other in Literary Structure*. Translated by Yvonne Freccero. Baltimore: Johns Hopkins Press, 1965.

———. "De l'expérience romanesque au mythe oedipien." *Critique* 222 (November 1965): 899–924.

———. *La violence et le sacré*. Paris: Grasset, 1972.

Giudice, Gaspare. *Pirandello*. Turin: UTET, 1963.

Gnisci, Armando. *Scrittura e struttura*. Rome: Silva, 1970.

Goffman, Ervin. *Asylums: Essays on the Social Situation of Mental Patients and Other Inmates*. Chicago: Aldine, 1961.

———. *Stigma: Notes on the Management of Spoiled Identity*. Englewood Cliffs: Prentice-Hall, 1963.

Golino, Enzo. "Con Priapo a Palazzo Venezia." *L'espresso*, August 13, 1967, p. 19.

Gozzano, Guido. "Guerra di spettri." Edited by Franco Contorbia. *Il lettore di provincia* 3 (December 1970): 14–24.

Gramsci, Antonio. *Letteratura e vita nazionale*. Turin: Einaudi, 1952.

Groddeck, Georg. *Psychoanalytische Schriften zur Psychosomatik*. Wiesbaden: Niedermayer, 1964.

Guarino, Pietro. "A proposito della 'conversione' verghiana." *Belfagor* 22, no. 2 (March 1967): 186–194.

Guglielmi, Guido. *Letteratura come sistema e come funzione*. Turin: Einaudi, 1967.

Guglielminetti, Marziano. *Struttura e sintassi del romanzo italiano del primo Novecento*. Milan: Silva, 1965.

Hamsun, Knut. *Psychologie und Dichtung*. Stuttgart: Kohlhammer, 1964.

Heller, Erich. *The Artist's Journey into the Interior*. New York: Random House, 1965.

Isenghi, Mario. "Borgese, Jahier e la guerra." *Quaderni piacentini* 5, no. 27 (June 1966): 80–90.

Jelly, Oliver. "Fiction and Illness." *A Review of English Literature* 3, no. 1 (January 1962): 80–89.

Jonard, Norbert. *Italo Svevo et la crise de la bourgeoisie européenne.* Paris: Les Belles Lettres, 1969.

Jung, Carl Gustav. *Psychological Types.* Translated by H. Godwin Baynes. New York: Harcourt, Brace & Co., 1926.

Kermode, Frank. *The Sense of an Ending.* New York: Oxford, 1968.

Klibanski, Raymond; Erwin Panofsky; and Fritz Saxl. *Saturn and Melancholy: Studies in the History of Natural Philosophy, Religion and Art.* London: Nelson, 1964.

Lacan, Jacques. *Écrits.* Paris: Seuil, 1967.

Laín Entralgo, Pedro. *La empresa de ser hombre.* 2d ed. Madrid: Taurus, 1963.

Laing, Ronald D. *The Politics of Experience.* New York: Pantheon, 1967.

———. *Self and Others.* 2d ed. New York: Pantheon, 1970.

Lavagetto, Mario. "Il dottor Freud fra scienza e letteratura." *Paragone* 21, no. 246 (August 1970): 44–85.

Leone De Castris, Arcangelo. *Italo Svevo.* Pisa: Nistri Lischi, 1959.

———. *Storia di Pirandello.* Bari: Laterza, 1962.

Luckmann, Thomas. *See* Berger, Peter L.

Lugnani, Lucio. *Pirandello: Letteratura e teatro.* Florence: La Nuova Italia, 1970.

Lukács, Georg. *The Meaning of Contemporary Realism.* Translated by John and Necke Mander. London: Merlin Press, 1963.

———. *Schriften zur Literatursoziologie.* Neuwied am Rhein: Luchterhand, 1963.

Luperini, Romano. *Pessimismo e verismo in Giovanni Verga.* Padua: Liviana, 1968.

Luti, Giorgio. *Italo Svevo e altri saggi sulla letteratura italiana del primo Novecento.* Milan: Lerici, 1962.

Macchia, Giovanni. *La caduta della luna.* Milan: Mondadori, 1973.

Macksey, Richard A., ed. *Velocities of Change: Critical Essays from MLN.* Baltimore: Johns Hopkins Press, 1974.

———, and Eugenio Donato, eds. *The Languages of Criticism and the Sciences of Man: The Structuralist Controversy.* Baltimore: Johns Hopkins Press, 1970.

Madrignani, Carlo. *Capuana e il naturalismo.* Bari: Laterza, 1970.

Maier, Bruno, ed. *Lettere a Svevo.* Milan: Dall'Oglio, 1973.

Mann, Thomas. *Essays.* Translated by H. T. Lowe-Porter. New York: Vintage, n.d.

Marañon, Gregorio. *El Greco y Toledo.* 4th ed. Madrid: Espasa-Calpe, 1963.

Mariani, Gaetano. *Storia della Scapigliatura.* Caltanissetta and Rome: Sciascia, 1967.

Masiello, Vitilio. *Verga tra ideologia e realtà.* Bari: De Donato, 1970.

Materassi, Mario. "Il pipistrello nel frigorifero." *Il Ponte* 28, nos. 4–5 (April–May 1972): 650–664.

Maxia, Sandro. *Lettura di Italo Svevo.* Padua: Liviana, 1965.

Michelstaedter, Carlo. *Opere.* Florence: Sansoni, 1958.

Milano, Paolo. "Opere d'immaginazione di un grande critico." *L'espresso,* August 16, 1970, p. 19.

————. "Ritocchi alla vita di Franz Kafka." *L'espresso,* September 15, 1968, p. 19.

Miller, J. Hillis. *The Disappearance of God.* Cambridge, Mass.: Harvard University Press, 1963.

Minerbi Treitel, Renata. "Zeno Cosini: The Meaning behind the Name." *Italica* 48, no. 2 (Summer 1971): 234–245.

Montale, Eugenio, and Italo Svevo. *Lettere, con gli scritti di Montale su Svevo.* Bari: De Donato, 1966.

Moravia, Alberto. "Il seduttore gioca con la morte." *L'espresso,* May 5, 1968, p. 22.

Musumarra, Carmelo. *Verga minore.* Pisa: Nistri-Lischi, 1965.

Novalis. *Schriften.* 3 vols. Berlin: Reimer, 1837–1846.

Pacifici, Sergio, ed. *From Verismo to Experimentalism.* Bloomington: Indiana University Press, 1969.

Pampaloni, Geno. "Italo Svevo." In *Il Novecento,* vol. 9 of *Storia della letteratura italiana,* edited by Emilio Cecchi and Natalino Sopegno, pp. 493–532. Milan: Garzanti, 1969.

————. "Quando cala il voltaggio." *La fiera letteraria,* August 31, 1967, p. 19.

Panofsky, Erwin. *The Life and Art of Albrecht Dürer.* Princeton: Princeton University Press, 1955.

————. *See* Klibanski, Raymond.

Parise, Goffredo. *L'assoluto naturale.* Milan: Feltrinelli, 1967.

Pautasso, Sergio. *Le frontiere della critica.* Milan: Rizzoli, 1972.

Pavese, Cesare. *The Burning Brand.* Translated by A. E. Murch. New York: Walker, 1961.

————. *Selected Letters.* Translated by A. E. Murch. London: Owen, 1969.

Peckham, Morse. *Beyond the Tragic Vision.* New York: Braziller, 1962.

————. *Man's Rage for Chaos: Biology, Behavior, and the Arts.* New York: Schocken, 1967.

————. *Romanticism: The Culture of the 19th Century.* New York: Braziller, 1965.

————. *The Triumph of Romanticism.* Columbia: University of South Carolina Press, 1970.

Pfohl, Russell. "Imagery as Disease in *Senilità.*" *MLN* 76, no. 2 (February 1961): 143–150.

Pirandello, Luigi. *The Late Mattia Pascal.* Translated by William Weaver. Garden City, N.Y.: Doubleday, 1964.

————. *Naked Masks: Five Plays.* Edited by Eric Bentley. New York: Dutton, 1952.

————. *Novelle per un anno.* 4th ed. "Presentazione" by Corrado Alvaro. Milan: Mondadori, 1962.

————. *The Old and the Young.* Translated by C. K. Scott-Moncrieff. New York: Dutton, 1928.

————. *One, None and a Hundred-thousand.* Translated by S. Putnam. New York: Dutton, 1933.

————. *Saggi, poesie, scritti vari.* Milan: Mondadori, 1960.

————. *Tutti i romanzi.* 2d ed. Milan: Mondadori, 1959.

Piro, Sergio. *Il linguaggio schizofrenico.* Milan: Feltrinelli, 1967.

Piromalli, Antonio. *Saggi critici di storia letteraria.* Florence: Olschki, 1967.

Porcelli, Bruno. "L'evoluzione dell'ideologia e della narrativa sveviane." *Problemi* 17–18 (1969): 767–782.

Praz, Mario. *The Romantic Agony.* Translated by Angus Davidson. 2d ed. London and New York: Oxford, 1970.

Pucci, Pietro. "Lingua e dialetto in Pasolini e in Gadda." *Società* 14, no. 2 (March–April 1958): 381–398.

————. "The Obscure Sickness." *Italian Quarterly* 11, no. 42 (Fall 1967): 43–62.

Raffa, Piero. *Avanguardia e realismo.* Milan: Rizzoli, 1967.

Ragusa, Olga. "Gadda, Pasolini, and Experimentalism: Form or Ideology?" In *From Verismo to Experimentalism,* edited by Sergio Pacifici, pp. 239–269. Bloomington: Indiana University Press, 1969.

————. *Verga's Milanese Tales.* New York: Vanni, 1964.

Raimondi, Ezio. "Gabriele D'Annunzio." In *Il Novecento,* vol. 9 of *Storia della letteratura italiana,* edited by Emilio Cecchi and Natalino Sapegno, pp. 1–84. Milan: Garzanti, 1969.

————. *Metafora e storia: Studi su Dante e Petrarca.* Turin: Einaudi, 1970.

————. *Politica e commedia: Dal Beroaldo al Machiavelli.* Bologna: Il Mulino, 1972.

————. "Symbolic Criticism." In *Velocities of Change,* edited by Richard A. Macksey, pp. 118–137. Baltimore: Johns Hopkins University Press, 1974.

Ramat, Raffaello. *Ragionamenti morali e letterari.* Bari: Laterza, 1945.

Raschini, M. A. *Carlo Michelstaedter.* Milan: Marzorati, 1965.

Rimanelli, Giose. "Federigo Tozzi: Misfit and Master." *Italian Quarterly* 14, no. 56 (Spring 1971): 29–76.

Rimini, Ruggero. "Un inedito di Svevo." *Belfagor* 26, no. 5 (September 1971): 599–600.

Risset, Jacqueline. "Carlo Emilio Gadda ou La philosophie à l'envers." *Critique* 282 (November 1970): 944–951.

Rizzo, Gino. "Luigi Pirandello in Search of a Total Theatre." *Italian Quarterly* 12, no. 45 (Summer 1968): 3–26.

Robinson, Paula. "*Senilità*: The Secret of Svevo's Weeping Madonna." *Italian Quarterly* 14, no. 55 (Winter 1971 [1970]): 61–84.

Rof Carballo, Juan. *Medicina y actividad creadora.* Madrid: Revista de Occidente, 1964.

Roscioni, Gian Carlo. "La conclusione della 'Cognizione del dolore.' " *Paragone* 238 (December 1969): 86–99.

———. *La disarmonia prestabilita: Studio su Gadda.* Turin: Einaudi, 1969.

Rosolato, Guy. "Étude des perversions sexuelles à partir du fétichisme." In *Le désir et la perversion,* pp. 7–52. Paris: Seuil, 1967.

Ruitenbeck, Hendrich M., ed. *Psychoanalysis and Literature.* New York: Dutton, 1964.

Russo, Luigi. *Giovanni Verga.* Bari: Universale Laterza, 1966.

Saccone, Eduardo. *Commento a "Zeno": Saggio sul testo di Svevo.* Bologna: Il Mulino, 1973.

———. "Furbank su Svevo." *MLN* 83, no. 1 (January 1968): 126–136.

———. "Il primo racconto di Italo Svevo." *Filologia e letteratura* 45 and 46 (1966): 93–112 and 201–218.

———. "*Senilità* di Italo Svevo: Dalla 'impotenza del privato' alla 'ansiosa speranza.' " *MLN* 82, no. 1 (January 1967): 1–55.

———. "Svevo, Zeno e la psicanalisi." *MLN* 85, no. 1 (January 1970): 67–82.

Sainte-Beuve, Charles Augustin. *Causeries du Lundi.* 15 vols. Paris: Garnier, 1852.

Salinari, Carlo. *Miti e coscienza del decadentismo italiano.* Milan: Feltrinelli, 1962.

Sapegno, Natalino. *See* Cecchi, Emilio.

Savarese, Gennaro. "Scoperta di Schopenhauer e crisi del naturalismo nel primo Svevo." *La Rassegna della letteratura italiana* 75, no. 3 (September–December 1971): 411–431.

Saxl, Fritz. *See* Klibanski, Raymond.

Scrivano, Riccardo. "Il Verga tra Scapigliatura e verismo." *Belfagor* 20, no. 6 (November 1965): 652–663.

Segre, Cesare. *I segni e la critica: Fra strutturalismo e semiologia.* Turin: Einaudi, 1969.

————. *See* Corti, Maria.

Sewell, Elizabeth. *The Orphic Voice: Poetry and Natural History.* London: Routledge & Kegan Paul, 1960.

Silone, Ignazio. *La scuola dei dittatori.* Milan: Mondadori, 1962.

Solmi, Sergio. *Scritti leopardiani.* Milan: All'insegna del pesce d'oro, 1969.

Sontag, Susan. *Against Interpretation.* New York: Farrar, Straus & Giroux, 1966.

Spinazzola, Vittorio. "Verismo e positivismo artistico." *Belfagor* 25, no. 3 (May 1970): 247–276.

Starobinski, Jean. *A History of Medicine.* Translated by Bernard C. Swift. New York: Hawthorn, 1964.

————. *La relation critique.* Paris: Gallimard, 1971.

Svevo, Italo. *As a Man Grows Older.* Translated by Beryl De Zoete. New York: New Directions, n.d.

————. *Commedie.* Milan: Dall'Oglio, 1969.

————. *Confessions of Zeno.* Translated by Beryl De Zoete. New York: Vintage, 1958.

————. *Epistolario.* Milan: Dall'Oglio, 1966.

————. *Further Confessions of Zeno.* Translated by Ben Johnson and Peter N. Furbank. Berkeley: University of California Press, 1970.

————. *A Life.* Translated by Archibald Colquhoun. New York: Knopf, 1963.

————. *Racconti. Saggi. Pagine sparse.* Milan: Dall'Oglio, 1969.

Sypher, Wylie. *Rococo to Cubism.* New York: Vintage, 1963.

Tarchetti, Igino Ugo. *Tutte le opere.* 2 vols. Bologna: Cappelli, 1967.

Trilling, Lionel. *The Liberal Imagination.* New York: The Viking Press, 1950.

Venè, Gian Franco. *Il capitale e il poeta.* Milan: Sugar, 1972.

————. *Pirandello fascista.* Milan: Sugar, 1971.

Veneziani Svevo, Livia. *Vita di mio marito.* Trieste: Edizioni dello Zibaldone, 1958.

Verga, Giovanni. *The House by the Medlar Tree.* Translated by Raymond Rosenthal. New York: Signet, 1964.

————. *Mastro-don Gesualdo.* Translated by D. H. Lawrence. New York: Grove Press, 1955.

————. *Una peccatrice e altri romanzi.* 3d ed. Milan: BMM, 1965.

Verri, Antonio. *Michelstaedter e il suo tempo.* Ravenna: Longo, 1969.

Vicentini, Claudio. *L'estetica di Pirandello.* Milan: Mursia, 1970.

Virtanen, Reino. "Claude Bernard and the History of Ideas." In *Claude*

Bernard and Experimental Medicine, edited by Maurice B. Visscher and Francisco Grande. Cambridge, Mass.: Schenkman, 1967.

Vittorini, Elio. *Conversation in Sicily*. Translated by Wilfrid David. Harmondsworth: Penguin, 1961.

———. *Le due tensioni*. Milan: Il Saggiatore, 1967.

Weigand, Hermann J. *Thomas Mann's Novel Der Zauberberg: A Study*. New York: Appleton-Century, 1933.

Whyte, L. L. *The Unconscious before Freud*. New York: Doubleday Anchor, n.d.

Wilden, Anthony. "Death, Desire and Repetition in Svevo's *Zeno*." *MLN* 84, no. 1 (January 1969): 98–119.

Woolf, Virginia. *Collected Essays*. 4 vols. London: Hogarth Press, 1967.

INDEX